Another River to Cross

Charles Johnson

Treasure House

An Imprint of

Destiny Image® Publishers, Inc.

P.O. Box 310

Shippensburg, PA 17257-0310

"For where your treasure is, there will your heart be also."
Matthew 6:21

ISBN 0-7684-3002-X
Library of Congress Catalog Card Number 2002-141109

For Worldwide Distribution
Printed in the U.S.A.

This book and all other Destiny Image, Revival Press, MercyPlace,
Fresh Bread, Destiny Image Fiction, and Treasure House books
are available at Christian bookstores and distributors worldwide.

For a U.S. bookstore nearest you, call **1-800-722-6774**.
For more information on foreign distributors, call **717-532-3040**.
Or reach us on the Internet:
www.destinyimage.com

ENDORSEMENTS

We are two among the countless multitudes who have been blessed by the music of Charles Johnson. His lyrics are simple, yet profound, and his style of singing clearly communicates their meaning in an unforgettable manner. Learning the story behind the man makes us appreciate him even more, not only as an anointed singer, but also as an extraordinary individual. We want to live next to him in heaven, just to get the musical overflow.

—Pat and Shirley Boone

This book not only tells one of the most thrilling and inspiring stories I have ever read, but it also contains clear and valuable teachings that touch all areas of life, illustrating them with unforgettable personal experiences. Don't wait until a late hour to start reading it because you won't be able to put it down.

—Gavin MacLeod

Reading the wit and wisdom of Charles Johnson's Granny brought me wonderful memories of my "Granny" on *The Beverly Hillbillies*.

And I couldn't help but think of "Ole Duke" when I read the hilarious account of Shep at the revival meeting. This entertaining book will make you laugh; it will make you cry; it will make you sing; but above all, it will make you want to live a better life. Y'all better read this book, you hear!

—Donna Douglas
"Elly May Clampett" of *The Beverly Hillbillies*

Throughout human history man has captured the rich essence of his experience in folklore, stories, and tales that enrich the lives of succeeding generations. *Another River to Cross* is destined to be one of them and should be read by everyone everywhere. This is a gripping and inspiring story of the majesty of the human spirit destined to take you across the rivers in your life.

—Dr. Myles Munroe
President
Bahamas Faith Ministries Int'l
Nassau, Bahamas

The legacy that Charles Johnson received and shares with us is of epic proportions. This book shows what God can do through an ordinary person who answers His call in unswerving obedience, and it challenges readers to develop to the fullest possible extent the abilities God has given them.

—Pat Robertson

This book cannot fail to thrill, encourage, and inspire anyone who, like Charles Johnson, is willing to be a committed vessel fit for God's use. The unforgettable story of his grandmother will leave without excuse those who say they can accomplish nothing because of low birth, lack of education and money, or other unfavorable circumstances. While *Another River to Cross* entertains, it also instructs, and you will consult its pages often for biblical principles to apply to your own circumstances.

—Rosey Grier

Just as Charles Johnson, I know what it is to pursue God's calling from humble beginnings, and both of us can testify that God is faithful to honor the commitment of a person intent on fulfilling His will in the strength of His Spirit. This book is a powerful witness to what God can accomplish through anyone, no matter how insignificant, who is completely dedicated to realizing a vision received from God, no matter how staggering that vision may seem.

—David Yonggi Cho

Seldom has a book stirred me as did *Another River to Cross*, and if it impacts you as it did me, then you won't rest on your past accomplishments, but you will reach higher and farther. This book shows that even the best can be better, the strongest can be stronger, and the greatest can be greater. Charles Johnson is a living demonstration that regardless of what God calls us to do, we are responsible to do it, and we can do it in the strength of our commitment and the resources He provides.

—Dottie Rambo

Another River to Cross provides more than entertaining and inspiring reading. In a simple and colorful style it presents timeless biblical truths. It especially gives a striking depiction of the principle of Seed Faith that I fervently preach and diligently practice. God is still multiplying the seed planted by an illiterate slave woman who had the wisdom to regard her greatest need as God's greatest opportunity and the courage to entrust everything she had to Him.

—Oral and Evelyn Roberts

Charles Johnson is a giant unparalleled in the field of gospel music, and his story is just as amazing as the man himself. Never have I heard of a more indomitable spirit than that of his grandmother. The courage, faith and positive outlook presented in this book will be a beacon for people who are facing formidable barriers, regardless of their race or nationality. *Another River to Cross* is destined to take its place among the all-time favorites of those who appreciate traditional moral and spiritual values.

—Andraè Crouch

CONTENTS

PREFACE

Some people say I'm a "crossover" singer. I don't know exactly what that means, but I suspect it has something to do with the fact that nobody knows what peg to hang me on in the music industry. Used to be, when I was lead singer and songwriter with the Sensational Nightingales, my music was often classed as "soul" or "black gospel." But I never knew that the gospel came in different colors, one for black and one for white. I always thought that true gospel music rose up in the depths of the soul, so I never gave much attention to such labels.

Nowadays a lot of people describe my music as "southern gospel," usually with a bewilderment that equates a black southern gospel singer with Charley Pride singing country. Here again, I have to express my ignorance, wondering how geographical divisions can identify the gospel. And why do some people talk about "contemporary" gospel music, as though the gospel was different at an earlier time than it is now?

I know that all these labels have to do with different styles of music, but I don't bother about any of them. All I know is that I sing what I feel, and I feel what I sing, and it doesn't matter to me how it comes out, just as long as the message is right and the sound of it is good enough for people to want to hear it. My music is not my livelihood; it's my life, the visible and vocal expression of who I am, what I am, and what I believe. Music is as natural to me as it is to a songbird; and like the Lord did for psalmists and prophets (see Ps. 42:8; Is. 30:29), He gives me songs in the night. He sets me free to sing Heaven's song on earth. I can no more stop singing than I can stop breathing, and my last song will indeed be with my last breath.

I want to express my sincere appreciation to Javetta Saunders and Jerry Horner, without whose assistance this book would never have been written, and to my wife Annie, without whose love and companionship I would be an incomplete man. With unbounded joy I proudly dedicate this book to the memory of the two most influential people in my life—my mother and my grandmother.

FOREWORD

Although Javetta Saunders had known Charles Johnson through his music for quite a while, she first actually met him when she booked him for a concert in her hometown of Bonifay, Florida. At that time Charles expressed to Javetta and her husband his desire to write his life story, and she responded that I might be a good candidate to help him, since I had done similar projects. My first reaction when Javetta approached me about the matter was to question the identity of Charles Johnson and what he had done that would cause people to want to read about him. The fact that he was a widely recognized composer and singer of gospel music meant little to me. The only thing I knew about music was to stand during the playing of the national anthem, and the only singers I knew anything about revealed the generation of my youth—Eddie Fisher, the Ames Brothers, Nat King Cole, Joni James, and their contemporaries. My field is academics, theology to be exact; and everyone knows that the preacher regards music as a preliminary that needs to be finished as quickly as possible in order to get to the real reason for gathering together…and that's to hear the sermon.

So, not being an appreciative connoisseur of Southern Gospel music, which I later learned is the closest label to describe the type of music that Charles Johnson produces, I had never heard of the man. However, I fancy myself to be something of a writer, with several books to my credit, and I figured that I could surely write down a story if somebody told it to me. You are about to read the result of my effort. Before you begin, I want you to understand that all I have done is to help Charles say what he wanted to say. The book is appropriately written in the first person, because it contains words plumbed from the depths of his heart, primarily encouraged by Javetta Saunders in lengthy interview sessions over a period of several months.

Charles is indeed a communicator, but he communicates in the lyrics and melodies of songs, not in written prose. The most difficult part in the writing of this book was to get Charles to talk about himself, and to stay focused when he did so. We had to prime his pump to get the information we needed. It took me no time at all to realize that the idea of writing this book did not originate with him, but that he was simply responding to the requests of a host of people who loved his ministry.

I also discovered that I was dealing with a living legend, a man who for more than 40 years had been crisscrossing the country on more back roads than on superhighways, and who was better known to some people in other countries than is the president of the United States. When I saw the list of his appearances for the year, I couldn't believe that the human body could physically endure such a gruelling schedule. I'm speaking of an average of between 150 and 200 concerts during the year, most often with widely spaced distances between locations on consecutive days. And all his traveling has been by car or bus, to such places as Bean Blossom, Indiana; Tickfaw, Louisiana; and Talladega, Alabama. Of course, also listed are a lot of other places more recognizable.

I was halfway through the manuscript before I attended one of those concerts. For the first six months since my original contact with Charles I had been based in London, England, receiving information from him and Javetta by telephone, fax, and e-mail. But I needed much more. I had to feel what he felt and respond as his audience responded. So on the way to a teaching engagement in Singapore, I took the longer western route from London and made a side trip to Texarkana, Texas. There I spent most of the day with Charles before his concert that night. His weariness was obvious, for he and his group had made a long drive from a distant town in Arkansas where they had given a concert the previous night. Yet he had to be at peak form again in just a short while, with no opportunity to rest.

I arrived at the Texarkana College theater well before the Revivers' performance time. I wanted to observe the people, to talk to them and learn who they were and why they had come. I judged the attendance to be in the neighborhood of 1,800, and at least 95 percent of the people were casually dressed, middle-class whites, mostly from evangelical, Pentecostal, charismatic, and fundamentalist churches. I was genuinely surprised at the large number of young people. The evening was like a family gathering, with lots of hugging and backslapping. The people were there for a good time, and from the very first it was clear that they were not passive spectators to be entertained, but active participants in a joyful celebration of worship. And they were not disappointed.

Charles and the three young male vocalists and musicians who backed him were as crisp and fresh as though they had just arrived from a week's holiday at a Caribbean spa. Supercharged with divine energy, they elicited from the crowd various expressions of worship—clapping, shouting, singing, dancing, and swaying. There was never a lull. Performers and people were at a spiritual peak the entire time.

I don't know the jargon of the music trade, so I'm at a loss to give a professional description of what I heard that night. The adjective that I would choose to describe the music of Charles Johnson and the Revivers is *fluid*. Their voices and instruments blend in a harmonious precision, producing the flowing tones of smooth, soothing anointing oil. There are no rough edges. If their music were fabric, it would be silk. If it were wood, it would be a finely polished exquisite piece of furniture, simple but stately. If it were food, it would be the richest Devon cream or the sweetest clover honey. If it were machinery, it would be the hum of the most perfectly tuned and well-oiled Rolls-Royce engine.

The group has its own unique style, and I suppose Southern Gospel is the category nearest in kinship, but I'm not the one to say. Someone who knows the business may detect smatterings of rhythm and blues, soul, and traditional country. All I know is that to an untrained ear like mine it sounds good and it ministers to the soul, because Charles Johnson is not an entertainer; first and foremost he is a minister.

Thank you, Charles, for allowing me the privilege of telling your story. And thank you, Javetta Saunders, for putting together so many different strands of information, helping me to bring them into a coherent whole. Truly, you are the fragrance of the flower.

—Jerry Horner

INTRODUCTION

The account my husband and I were hearing from Charles Johnson over a leisurely dinner completely enraptured me. He had prefaced the story with a request that I help him write a book, and the story he told was in response to my question concerning the nature of the book. What you will read in *Another River to Cross* is an expansion of what Charles sketched that night. I knew then that the brief narrative that he shared with us had to be heard in its entirety, and by a much wider audience.

My introduction to Charles Johnson occurred around 1988, when my nine-year-old daughter, Rachel, was singing at a gospel concert in Pensacola, Florida, that featured several groups, including Charles and The Revivers. Although I thoroughly enjoyed their music, I attached no special significance to the occasion, especially since Rachel had been singing publicly since the age of five and had appeared with many noted singers. However, I was later to learn that what seemed to be only a chance encounter was actually a divine appointment.

Eleven years passed before I saw Charles again, but I had become increasingly acquainted with him through his recordings. God's anointing was not only present in his live performances, it was stamped indelibly upon electronic tape, and the music always inspired me. So when my pastor appointed me to plan a gospel concert as part of a fundraising drive for a new church building, I immediately determined to invite Charles Johnson and The Revivers.

When Charles came to my hometown of Bonifay, Florida, my husband and I hosted him at dinner. At that time I expressed my great appreciation for his music and revealed to him that I had already been promoting him. It was because of my recommendation that he and The Revivers had appeared on a telethon at my family's Christian television station in Orlando. I also shared with him some other promotions in which I had been involved. In response, he inquired about the possibility of my helping him produce some musical videos, which we have since accomplished. Then he confessed that for years he had longed to write a book, but needed the right person to help him. I told him that I knew the person.

The result of that conversation is in the pages of this book. After I told my friend, Dr. Jerry Horner, the captivating story that Charles related, he agreed to write the book, on the condition that I be responsible for providing him with material gleaned from conversations with Charles. I have read the resulting manuscript several times, and the story is just as compelling as the first time I heard it. I spent long hours in telephone interviews with Charles, gathering information to relate to Dr. Horner. Some of the accounts I heard touched me so deeply that I could respond only with weeping, while other reports fired me with uproarious hilarity. I still have the same reactions when I read the written narration. I thank Charles Johnson and I praise God for the opportunity to participate in the production of such a wonderful volume.

—Javetta Lora Saunders

CHAPTER ONE

REJECTING THE REJECTION

T here was nothing particularly unusual about the small procession of people making their way down the aisle of the auditorium that wintry day of 1962 in Oklahoma City. Most observers saw a few elderly black people led by the determined progress of an aged woman who was obviously the matriarch of the group. She was barely five feet tall and would hardly push the scales past the one hundred-pound mark, even while wearing her long black coat with its fake fur collar. Her erect carriage was almost regal as she walked with quick unfaltering steps that needed no assistance. Her sharp eyes surveyed the room without the aid of spectacles, missing nothing of interest. Perched on her head was a dainty wide brim hat that she wore like a crown, and it did not conceal the fact that her hair was luxuriantly full and only speckled with gray. The years had left her face remarkably unlined, and her skin had successfully resisted the leathering process that normally occurs with the passing of time. I was one of the few people present who knew that the skin on her shoulders and back was quite different, ridged with ancient scars resulting from beatings administered a hundred years earlier by a merciless slave owner trying to suppress her defiant spirit. I had been well acquainted with those scars since my earliest days, having viewed their ugliness and touched their harshness and heard stories of their origin. This woman was my sweet Granny, and at the age of 111 she had come to hear me sing professionally for the first time.

On the stage where I was helping to set up the equipment, I was overcome with all kinds of emotion at my first sight of this precious lady in eight years. I was riveted to the floor as wave after wave of love, joy, pride, and gratitude swelled over me. In a rush of release the emotional tide drove me off the platform and down the aisle to receive the long overdue embrace of the woman who taught me more about life and living than any other person on earth did. As our tears salted the sweetness of our kisses, memories scattered by years of neglect congregated in a heap to fill my soul. I honored her that night by pulling out all those memories to underscore the words of her favorite hymn, "Glory to His Name," which I sang with more fervor than ever before in tribute to her.

We have scant information about Granny's life prior to her slave years. All we know is that she and her twin sister were only about ten years old when treacherous slave traders deemed them strong enough to endure the rigors of a nightmarish journey across the Atlantic and bring a handsome price at the auction. So two terrified little girls had only each other as a source of comfort and courage as they were snatched from their family in the grassy plains of French West Africa and forced to share the brutal experience of countless others who had been shipped to America's Southland to maintain the lifeblood of the plantations. Fortunately, divine grace and kind years blotted out painful memories of the trip itself, for Granny spoke little of the horror it must have been. Perhaps she herself allowed pleasant memories of a faraway home deliberately to slip away, because even beautiful thoughts of lost things that can never be recovered can become bitter if one insists on holding onto the grief. But it was not Granny's nature to entomb herself in the dark vault of regretful self-pity. "Anybody what adds one day's misery to the next ain't gone to have room for today's joy," she used to say. Even though she couldn't read or write a single word, Granny knew the Bible through and through. She understood exactly what Jesus meant when He talked about trusting a loving Father instead of carrying today's worries into tomorrow and adding the expectation of tomorrow's problems to the burdens you already have today (see Mt. 6:34).

Granny was listed as "Anna" and her sister as "Sarah" on the roster of slaves to be sold in Louisiana. Whether or not the slave masters realized it, both names have strong biblical significance, quite appropriate to the two little girls. Anna was a prophetess who faithfully served the Lord and prophesied over the infant Jesus (see Lk. 2:36-38). Her name means "favor"; Granny, who also served the Lord, found favor as well. Sarah was the wife of Abraham and the mother of Isaac (see Gen. 21:1-3). Her name means "princess," and although our Sarah was a slave, she was royalty in God's sight. The biblical Anna and Sarah both lived long lives, and their namesakes both lived well past the age of 100.

Neither of the girls could understand a word of English, so their pleas went unheeded as men interested only in profit ignored their cries. After all, it wasn't as though these two little naked forms were considered precious children of God who had been ripped from the loving arms of grief-stricken parents. They were merely subhuman creatures whose only function was to serve superior masters. And so Anna and Sarah, who had shared life together since their common conception, were shamelessly sold to buyers representing different plantation owners. In their bewilderment, they could only shout vain words of hope to each other until distance took them out of range of sight and sound. The sisters, once inseparable, would not see each other again until a hundred years had passed. But through all of those hundred years, neither sister forgot, and neither one gave up hope.

Granny was taken to a farm near Anniston, Alabama, where she suffered the cruelty of harsh overseers until the savagery of the war that divided the nation was finally brought to an end. Even though she carried the ugly scars of her captivity until her death in 1966 at the age of 115, she never spoke a word of hatred against anyone who had wronged her. Her explanation was simple: "They beat the Lord Jesus a whole lot worse than they beat me, and He said we got to forgive people just like He did. Besides, the only one be hurt is the one who don't forgive, 'cause with all that bitterness in the heart there ain't no room for goodness and joy and peace. And it ain't worth losin' the joy of the Lord just so you can feel right about hatin' somebody." The conviction with which she spoke was so powerful and her logic so irresistibly simple that we could never forget the lessons she impressed upon us. Furthermore, the unsightly scars that corded her back became to me a source of pride, the symbol of a courageous spirit that perseveres against all hardships.

Like most other liberated slaves after the war, Granny had no choice but to continue in the only life she had known—working in the fields from sunrise to sundown. Only now in place of the sting of a whip, there was a small wage to be earned. In recounting those days, Granny spoke in a matter-of-fact manner. She could tell of happy occasions without romanticizing them to the extent that the former slaves involved appeared to be simple children without any care under the patronage of white benefactors who were once their benevolent masters, but who were now their protectors and providers. On the other hand, she could tell of difficulties without rancor and complaint. She never gave us reason to believe that she felt cheated in life or that the Lord had failed her. Her attitude made good sense: "Folks that sit around moanin' and groanin' about how they been wronged just usin' up good energy that could be put to use in gettin' them somewhere. You don't do nothin' but think about what happened to you in the past, you ain't got no time to think about what you can make happen in the future. A man tryin' to walk straight ahead while lookin' over his shoulder goin' bump into all kind of things and get nowhere. Me, I got too much to plan for and live for than to waste time worryin' about something already gone by."

She had an emphatic way of illustrating her points by telling the stories of biblical characters like Joseph, Moses, and Daniel, who came out of adverse circumstances to accomplish mighty deeds. From the way she talked about them, they seemed to be more like personal acquaintances rather than historical figures of ages past. Only much later did I understand that Granny's familiarity arose from a fellowship of experience. "It don't make no nevermind what man do," she said. "God got His own plans. Man do bad things, God turn them into good things. Just reject the rejection." As a child I understood how God overturned the evil that men intended into something good for His servants; but the most convincing evidence for me was Granny's own testimony of good coming out of evil. She praised God for everything, even for being uprooted from her African home and transported into a life of slavery. What good could come out of that? She explained that had she never left Africa she might never have heard of Jesus Christ and His salvation, and so she would have remained in the far worse slavery of paganism. "Man make me a slave," she declared, "but Jesus make me a free child of God." She went on to explain that had she never come to America as a slave, none of us children would have been born. Now that's something to think about!

Despite the bare livelihood the freed slaves managed to eke out of their meager income, they could make their own plans, move where and when they wanted to, and marry partners of their own choosing. So Granny married my grandfather Johnson, whom I never knew because of his death years before I was born. Together they had nine children—three boys and six girls, one of whom was my mother, Mamie.

The freedom that they enjoyed did not bring economic prosperity to most of the former slaves, and many realized that they were in worse shape than they were in their former bondage. So they dreamed dreams and prayed prayers for a better future. Finally, it appeared that their opportunity had come. There was talk of wonderful possibilities in Texas, with virgin farmland waiting to be tilled. A man by the name of Matt Reese was the driving force behind the prospective exodus to a place about which they knew nothing. It was a challenge even to consider leaving their homeland, because, however bleak and unpromising their condition was, as least they had the comfort of familiar surroundings. But Matt's persuasion was irresistible, and several families, including the Johnsons, agreed to join in the migration to a place where they supposedly could produce twice as much cotton with half the effort. To impoverished people who in bondage had enjoyed few personal belongings and in freedom possessed even less in the way of material things, the prospect of working their own land and harvesting their own crops seemed heavenly. Granny saw it as the Israelites departing Egypt for the Promised Land. As far as risking the unknown was concerned, I could imagine her declaring with a snort, "A turtle that don't stick his neck out ain't goin' nowhere!"

The Bible story Granny loved most, and never tired of hearing and retelling to her children, was how God enabled Moses to lead his fellow Hebrews from a land where they had known only oppression and hardship into a land that by contrast was a paradise. "Ain't goin' take no forty years to get there," she declared, " 'cause the Lord done already fit the battle for us. And we sho ain't goin' be like them that didn't believe Him. Ain't no ground goin' swallow me up, and 'sides, I ain't got no forty years to spare." Well, as a matter of fact, she had the years, destined to live another seventy or so, but she certainly didn't have the patience!

So it was that a miniature exodus took place scant years before the dawn of the twentieth century, consisting of a few families crowded in covered wagons with their meager possessions. The only additional things they took with them were bittersweet memories of survival during years of struggle working somebody else's land and seeing most of the fruit of their labor profiting the owners. No tears were shed as the wagon wheels rutted the red clay of Alabama at the beginning of a westward journey toward prosperity. My mother, just a tot at the time, was among the pilgrims.

CHAPTER TWO

FITTING INTO GOD'S MOLD

The enthusiasm of the newly planted settlers remained high, even when it became apparent that they had not discovered Eden. Regarding quality of life, as far as material things were concerned, there was little recognizable difference in what they found near Paris, Texas, and what they had left behind. The sun was just as hot, the winters were even colder, the labor was just as burdensome, and the material rewards were just as slight. However, there was a vast difference in the atmosphere in which they lived. In the Pine Creek bottomland of Lamar County they breathed the heady air of freedom. They had formed their own community, with its church and school, and with the dignity of planning their own future and the reality that hope of better things was more than a futile dream. So, even though most of them were still sharecropping, and even though the toil was just as hard as they had previously known, the sense of bondage was lifted and the burden of labor was lightened by the very love of it.

It was in that same setting that I was born almost 40 years later. By most standards, Granny was already ancient at the time, being about 80 years of age. If anyone had told her that she couldn't or shouldn't be doing the things she was doing at her age, it was obvious that she paid no attention. Not only did she keep house for her second husband, whom she married after the death of my grandfather, she still worked in the fields, tended a garden, and canned fruits and vegetables. She was an excellent seamstress, and every daughter and granddaughter in the family wore dresses that Granny made from Mother's Best flour sacks. To this day I can still hear the melodic hum of the old treadle sewing machine. Many nights that was the lullaby that cradled me to sleep.

Granny's passion, however, was quilting, and every scrap of cloth was thrust into her quilting bag, later to become part of a beautiful original tapestry. When she found time to make them, I don't know, but her matchless multicolored works of art are scattered across the country today. She never sold a single one of them; all were given to those whom she loved. It was her nature to give, and she taught us the rewards of giving. Her logic was simple: "The Bible say them what gives, gets. So when I give something away, I ain't lost it; it goin' come back to me, only a whole lot more." Having worked in the fields her whole life, she understood the principle that Jesus taught when He said, "Unless a grain of wheat falls into the ground and dies, it remains alone; but if it dies, it produces much grain" (Jn. 12:24). An unplanted seed is doomed to the barrenness of self-isolation, but the self-sacrifice of a seed that is planted and dies to itself brings forth a bountiful harvest. In the same way, a person who hoards his life will remain in the drab loneliness of selfishness, whereas the person who willingly gives of himself and his possessions has the satisfaction of blessing both others and himself immeasurably. Granny was never preachy about such things; she just practiced what she believed, acting out a sermon that was far more powerful than any spoken word.

Granny also was the unofficial midwife of the area, and practically every baby for miles around, black or white, was birthed with her assistance. Of course, she never had a moment's instruction in midwifery, having learned everything by observation and the personal experience of giving birth to nine children of her own. "Ain't nothing more natural," she said of childbirth. "It's the way of the Lord for all His creatures."

During all the births she attended, Granny never lost the wonder of a precious beautiful new life sucking air into its lungs for the first time. Not one baby whom she drew from a mother's womb left her arms without an earnest prayer for the newborn's health and dedication to the Lord. To her, life was a priceless gift from God, and children were treasures to be guarded and valued. She would have been horrified by the statistics concerning abortion and the casual attitude toward the murder of millions of innocent babies. It would have been unthinkable to her that any human being, civilized or not, Christian or pagan, would resort to such savagery. If she had the opportunity to testify concerning the subject, no one would be able to refute her logic or resist her impassioned pleas. It was no mystery to her when life began, and it was pointless to debate the issue. She was simple enough to believe what the Bible taught—that God knew the child in a past eternity and knit that little body together in the mother's womb (see Ps. 139:13-16). Anybody who contradicted that pronouncement by describing the pulsating presence in the womb as a blob of fatty tissue that can be cut out as though it was a tumor was not only a fool, but a blind ignoramus as well. I think God surely approves Granny's old-fashioned way of thinking over the views of the so-called enlightened sophisticates of today, who in reality are barbarous butchers.

My grandmother not only attended to physical needs at the time of childbirth; in addition, she functioned as a minister. She rejoiced with the family when the baby was healthy, and she brought comfort and gave instruction in those rare instances of stillbirth or deformity of some kind. Her compassion was unmistakably genuine as she served as the Lord's instrument of healing and restoration. Unfortunately, she missed my birth, having been called upon to attend someone else. She always expressed regret that she didn't have the privilege of bringing me into the world, but she jokingly admitted that the substitute did a "fair to middlin' " job.

I was born so far out in the country the sun rose between the place where we lived and the county seat of Paris. My earliest memories are of playing on the dirt floor of our cabin, with my mother hovering over a cast-iron woodstove. We had neither plumbing nor electricity. A coal oil lamp provided light, and our water came from a hand pump. A path led to a rickety outhouse conveniently supplied with an outdated Sears-Roebuck catalog. The only improvement after we moved to Sugar Hill was a floor. Everything else was the same. I could still lie in bed and see the stars through the roof. The windows were made with boards to keep the wolves outside.

My father left the family before I was born, and I never saw him until I was about 12 years old. My mother and her children retained the name Johnson, and I had only a casual relationship with my

Granny and Baby

father after our initial meeting. During the hard depression years, we led what would be regarded today as a dreary, austere, poverty-stricken routine, barely above the survival line. Mama worked in the cotton fields to keep me and my brother and three sisters fed and clothed. My sisters wore their flour-sack dresses, and A.J. and I didn't know that men and boys wore anything other than Big Chief overalls. The boys wore them long in the winter and with the legs cut off in the summer. We wore shoes from sometime in October until April, and then only out of the necessity caused by cold weather.

Washing and ironing was a weekly ritual that occupied two full days. On Monday we children pumped water and gathered wood for heating it outside in the big black kettle. The garments soaked in a galvanized tin tub filled with scalding water as Mama pulled them out one by one and attacked them with a vengeance, giving them a thorough and harsh rubbing on the scrub board. Homemade lye soap was the usual commodity in washing clothes. That stuff was so powerful that no germ could survive its acidic bite, and dirt didn't stand a chance. For that matter, neither did the skin on Mama's hands in a day when Playtex gloves were as unthinkable as home computers. Only occasionally did Mama experience the luxury of Oxydol or Rinso powdered soap on washdays. Giant bars of P & G soap were a staple in every house, including ours. They served to wash dishes, bodies, and clothes when lye soap was unavailable. Our clothes dryer consisted of the natural elements of sun and wind, producing a sweet-smelling cleansing effect on the clothes hung out to dry.

On Tuesdays Mama set up her ironing board within arm's reach of the wood cookstove. While the two flatirons were heating on top of the stove, she sprinkled the clothes and rolled them up, ready for ironing. She used one red-hot iron until it cooled, then used the other one while the first reheated. She stood by that stove most of the day, even in the summer. Sometimes it got so unbearably hot in the kitchen that flies soon learned not to invade it, because it cost them every bit of their energy trying to flit through the suffocating heat. I still think of Mama when I hear women complain of their back-breaking chore of putting laundry into automatic washers and dryers.

All of us children had our chores as well. We hated them, but we did them. I pumped water, split and ranked stove wood, chopped and picked cotton, slopped the hogs, tended the garden, and performed a variety of other assignments as a matter of routine. Of all of them, picking cotton was my favorite, not because I liked it, but because it brought in hard cash. I began in the fields as a toddler, mainly accompanying my mother, by pulling a flour sack that would take me all day to fill. Later, as I grew older, I graduated to a tow sack, and then finally to an abbreviated version of the adult sack. We would usually get in the field by sunrise, when the cotton was still wet with dew. It was worth getting soaked and chilled, because the first weigh-in would be at least one-half again as heavy. The sun dried out any hope of dew-soaked, heavier loads after that first one. By mid-morning the frosty chill of the dawn yielded to scorching heat as the sun blazed its fury on us. Early in the season our fingertips would split and start bleeding until they became calloused enough to withstand the pricks of sharp cotton bolls. Many times I thought of Granny doing all this with no reward except the tip of a whip if she didn't meet her expected quota. We stayed in the field until the last weigh-in at sunset. By then the mule-drawn wagon, reinforced with high sideboards, was filled with its white fluffy gold.

The cotton field wasn't all drudgery. Throughout the day there was plenty of conversation as we inched our way down the long straight rows. Invariably someone would start a song, and it would swell across the broad acres as others added their voices. At noon we had the luxury of resting in the shade of the nearest oak tree with a lunch that usually consisted of cold biscuits, tomatoes, and leftover beans, turnips, or potatoes. The more fortunate ones sometimes enjoyed potted meat, Vienna sausages, bologna, or some similar meat. But the greatest treat of all, the one that we most coveted, was an RC Cola and a Moon Pie. For ten cents we couldn't ask for anything better, not that I knew there was anything better.

The best part of the day, of course, was at the end, when we climbed the wagon and allowed our weary bodies to soak in the softness of the cotton we had complained about all day. Even after so many years I can still smell the scent of freshly picked cotton and think back on those hard times. I certainly don't have any desire to go back, but still I often regret that my children never had the experience of being perched atop a mountain of cotton that mules were straining to pull.

If farm owners in those days had been subjected to the same government regulations that are enforced today, none of us would have had those experiences, because no farmer could possibly have followed them. Nobody provided us with insurance and health care, safety equipment, retirement benefits, minimum wage guarantees, and sanitary facilities proportionate to the number of workers. When the natural functions of the body demanded attention, we headed for the cornfield or the bushes. We carried our lunch in a tin lard bucket and our water in a gallon jug. We figured nobody owed us anything that we didn't earn, and there sure weren't any welfare or food stamp programs that we could claim. We worked hard, but it was with dignity, and we were better for it. It seems to me that government bureaucracy has done more harm than good. I honestly believe that many farms were abandoned and many small businesses shut down because the owners were buried under pointless paperwork and financially oppressed by absurd and unreasonable federal regulations.

We did have time to play, even though I don't recall ever having a store-bought toy or game as a child. We invented our own games and manufactured our own toys. People today don't know what marvelous things one's imagination can produce or what modes of entertainment an old tire can provide or the exhilaration of chasing after a metal hoop pushed along by a flattened tin can nailed to the end of a stick. Without television to imprison us, we children frolicked outdoors for hours playing such games as red rover, hopscotch, leap frog, sling tail, mumble peg, and the like. In addition, there was always swimming and fishing and hunting.

One day my Uncle Lish, Aunt Julie's husband, wanted to join in the fun down at the creek where we were skinny-dipping. We would make like Tarzan by swinging over the creek on a rope dangling from a tree limb and let go at the exact moment to hit the water below. The only problem was that Uncle Lish swam like a rock. So he fashioned a flotation device consisting of two gallon jugs tied to each ankle. Things went great as he gave the mandatory Tarzan yell during his graceful swing over the creek. He was less graceful as he wildly flailed the air on the downward plunge into the water, but fortunately he had let go of the rope at the precise moment to hit the creek midstream. Now ordinarily a body would emerge from the depths of the water headfirst. But all we saw were four jugs and the soles of two feet, which we correctly figured belonged to Uncle Lish, the rest of whom was hanging upside down with his head scraping the bottom. He was a mite waterlogged by the time we managed to drag him ashore. We encouraged him to give it another try, this time with the jugs tied around his neck, but he declined. By the way, this was the same Uncle Lish who demonstrated to us one time the proper way to make like a paratrooper by jumping off the top of a barn with an umbrella. He was laid up for quite a spell, and we boys decided it would be safer to make like Tex Ritter or Gene Autry.

We had no option when it came to going to church. I don't know who invoked the most fear in us—the Lord, Mama, or Granny. The church nursery was the spot on the bench next to Mama, and if I tried to crawl out of the nursery I would live to regret it. I know, because I did try once, and Mama caused me to regret it to this day.

Church services were always lively and exuberant, with enthusiastic singing, fiery and fervent preaching, and lots of shouting. But there was one service in particular that folks who were there still talk about. Every summer, usually in August after the crops were laid by, we had a revival meeting, usually lasting two weeks. In those days social life revolved around the home, the church, the school, and the general store. So when there was a revival, folks came. Now a lot of the men, mostly the unchurched ones, wouldn't come inside, but stayed outside where they could smoke, tell stories, and socialize. It was the last night of the meeting, the climax of everything, the moment toward which the whole revival had been building. Well, the devil evidently got riled up at the preacher for talking about him the way he did and decided to demonstrate the hell the preacher had been trying to describe.

Spud Adams (I never knew his real name) had a huge old mongrel dog that followed him everywhere, even to church. Nobody minded, because the dog never caused any trouble. He just plopped on the floor under the bench where Spud was sitting, and there was not a sound from him all through the service—except this night.

The preacher had ardently hollered his lungs out and made an impassioned appeal for sinners to repent. It's strange how sometimes events can come together just at the precise time to set off a chain reaction that can have momentous results, whether disastrous or otherwise. It's almost like they are designed that way, destined so to speak. This was one of those moments.

The preacher told the congregation to stand and sing while mourners came forward. Who knows what force prompted old Shep to swish his tail at that second? Surely it had to be the same compulsion that prompted Sister Thomkins, all 300 pounds of her, to sit on the bench directly behind Spud. And that same force must have guided Sister Thomkins' foot, generously endowed in size, in descending to the floor at a time to coincide with the movement of Shep's tail. The result of an encounter like that is inevitable. The bloodcurdling shriek that the unsuspecting and innocent dog screamed when 300 pounds crushed the tender tip of his tail put the fear of hell into the whole congregation.

What followed was complete bedlam. In a split second old Shep leaped in terror-filled pain, fighting to get away from his torment. His struggles toppled Spud's bench backward, knocking over the row of people behind him, who in turn fell over the next row, creating a domino effect of tumbled bodies all the way to the last row. Meanwhile, Shep had managed to disentangle himself and was painfully running around inside the building, yelping for all he was worth. All this happened in seconds, and what with all the fallen bodies and shouting, the rest of the congregation thought the Spirit had come down, and they started doing some jumping and shouting themselves. People started running to the altar and falling to their knees.

The best part of all was that the socializing reprobates outside got so curious about the noise they had to check out what was going on. The people inside concluded the conviction was so great, it had driven the sinners in, and before the outsiders knew what was happening they had been pushed to the altar. They never stood a chance as the saints prayed them through. I reckon I was the only one who noticed as Shep finally found the door and tore out for home, howling all the way.

Everybody agreed that it was the best revival they could remember. What difference does it make how it came about? God can use any instrument. If He can speak through Balaam's donkey, can't He speak through old Shep?

Granny never entered a church door without her big Bible. Somebody asked her once why she always carried the Bible, when she couldn't read it. In reply she told the story of an old deaf slave who attended church faithfully. When somebody asked him why he sat through hymns and sermons he couldn't hear, he responded that he just wanted the devil to know whose side he was on. In similar fashion, Granny explained, "The Bible be the sword of the Lord, and I ain't goin' do no fightin' with the devil without the only weapon goin' strike him down."

She couldn't read it, but she knew it from Genesis to Revelation, and she understood what it meant. She made certain that somebody read to her every day, and she taught me more about the Bible than any seminary professor could have. I especially learned, both by her teaching and her example, the value of faith. Her favorite doctrinal topic was the second coming of Jesus, and I wonder sometimes if part of the explanation of her long life was her determined effort to live until the Lord returned. I have in my possession today the tattered Bible that she prized so much, and it means more to me than any award and honor I have received.

Granny was quite strict in all spiritual matters, especially prayer, and she tolerated no foolishness in things of the Lord. She herself was a praying person, and she would always gather her grandchildren together and pray for them one by one. She expected us to pray also. We dared not take a bite of food without first giving thanks, and we knew better than to sneak into bed at night without saying our prayers. Offenders could expect a blistered bottom. If I needed God I would go to my grandmother, and I would never be disappointed. I have never forgotten her counsel, more of which I'll share later.

As I've mentioned, we lived far out in the country—so far that I never even actually saw or heard a train until I was six years old. I had only heard stories about them and seen pictures of them. So I kept begging and pestering Mama until she finally consented to take me to see the train in Paris. The sight of such a vehicle! Just the monstrous size of it exceeded all my expectations. I was entranced by the magnificence of the powerful locomotive, with hissing steam and billowy clouds of black smoke and the rhythmic click-clack of its wheels racing along the track.

Unfortunately, the locomotive had a steam whistle, and nobody had forewarned me. Evidently the engineer meant to give a friendly greeting to the little black boy clutching his mother's hand while watching with fascination the onrushing train, so he gave a long pull on the whistle. That must have been the only time in my life that I've had white skin. I had never heard such an ungodly piercing scream in all my life. I took off running after I landed from the two feet in the air I had jumped. Mama chased me for two blocks before I stopped crying enough to heed her pleas to stop. Only then did I discover that the whistle had scared the pee out of me, and the evidence was plain to see.

In all my years of childhood, I don't recall seeing a doctor once. Again, because we lived a distance out in the country, it wasn't easy to see a doctor like you do today every time you have the sniffles. We weren't able to afford medical care anyway. Naturally, Granny was the medical supervisor in our region, and except for surgical procedures she could probably diagnose and prescribe as well as any doctor or pharmacist. The prescription part was easy, because it was the same for most common ills. Castor oil supposedly was the best remedy for bodily ailments. Just cleanse the system and everything else that wasn't meant to be there would go as well. Black Draught, Syrup Pepsin, and Grove's Chill Tonic all had their occasional uses, but the old standby was castor oil. I don't believe Granny was ever without a bottle of the foul liquid, ready for any emergency. It was as much a part of her bag as cosmetics are for an ordinary woman.

One day walking home from school, I couldn't resist the temptation to raid a sweet potato patch. I don't know how many I ate, down to the roots, but it was enough to present me with a colossal stomachache. I felt as though a thousand demons were using my poor bloated belly as their playground, leapfrogging over each other and competing for the somersault championship. My insides were cramping so painfully I was afraid I would die. Before long I was afraid I wouldn't die. When Granny showed up I knew the inevitable was going to happen. There was no preliminary counseling, no attempt to get me to cooperate, because experience had already proved how futile it would be. Mama held me down by the wrists and Granny pinched my nose with one hand, while her other hand directed the biggest spoon I had ever seen toward my screaming mouth. It surely had to contain a pint of the dreaded castor oil. I lasted as long as I could hold my breath, then I had no choice but to open my mouth. Granny knew from long years of practice that she had only a fraction of a second to act before I could take another breath and seal the target again. Her timing was perfect, as usual. With one smooth continuous motion she poured the vile stuff down my throat and with her hand clamped my mouth shut. Despite my best efforts, I managed to expel only a few drops. I had to swallow before I suffocated or drowned, whichever came first.

The effect was almost immediate. The imagined demons were swimming for their lives, turning my insides into a boiling, churning cauldron. The ultimate and desired result soon followed. With lightning speed I had never before exhibited, I raced for the outhouse and its blissful promise of relief. There I spent most of the next few hours, during which time the Sears-Roebuck catalog got progressively thinner. I still get a queasy feeling when I eat sweet potatoes.

For the most part, we were self-sufficient in providing our food, and it was usually plentiful. Sometimes our needs were met through the bartering system; for example, we traded butter or milk for meat. Everyone had a huge garden that assured us of plenty of fresh or home-canned vegetables the year round. We supplemented what we grew with what we gathered from the wild, such as greens, grapes, nuts, berries, roots, and honey. I especially have vivid memories of picking blackberries, and for more reasons than the lingering taste of the most delicious pies and cobblers imaginable. Forget the briars that drew blood from every inch of exposed skin. Far worse than that were the chiggers that burrowed into any part of the skin, from the scalp to the toes.

Now if you don't know what chiggers are, consider yourself blessed. These tiny red bugs, practically invisible to the naked eye, prefer the human body to the grass and foliage where they normally dwell. There was no immunity from the scourge of these pests, which found their way even through clothing, and it's difficult to fight what you can't see. Evidently they had a special fondness for blackberry patches and the pickers who got trapped in the close confines of the entangling vines. They delighted in colonizing those defenseless bodies. By the time we got home and rinsed ourselves off, it was too late. The army of vicious little creatures had already established their positions under our skin, and no amount of vigorous scrubbing would dislodge them. While they would dig in anywhere on the body, they especially favored the ankles, the scrotum, and the scalp. The itching caused by scores of little red hills resulting from the chigger bites was maddening, and our constant scratching made the infection worse, sometimes causing open sores that left scars when they finally healed. I never eat a blackberry without shuddering at the thought of chiggers.

We drank milk straight from the cow, and we ate piles of freshly churned butter generously applied to hot biscuits or cornbread. We had plenty of eggs and chickens to eat, as well as pork and occasionally goat. To what we raised domestically we added fish and wild game, usually squirrel, possum, coon, rabbit, and fowl, such as ducks and turkeys. Hog-killing time, usually in November at the first serious cold spell, was a community event. Nothing about the pigs was wasted, not even the bristles. Even the feet, the ears, the tail, and the skin were preserved for consumption, as were internal organs such as the brains and the liver. And I won't bother describing chitterlings (or chittlings, as we said), except to say that they were the unmentionable parts of the pig.

You have probably heard of sheep being led to the slaughter, but I doubt if there is any sight or sound quite like pigs being driven to the slaughter. After herding the unsuspecting creatures together, the men would hit them between the eyes with a sledgehammer, with the intent, of course, of killing them instantly with a powerful blow.

Now Grandpa Hurd, Granny's second husband, was a gentle Methodist preacher who tried not to offend anybody, whether human or beast. But on one occasion he succeeded in getting a big boar pretty riled. Well into his eighties, Rev. Hurd didn't have the agility, strength, and eyesight that he once had, as he lifted the heavy hammer and aimed for the head of the biggest hog in the lot. However, the swine wasn't of a mind just to stand there and take it, and the reverend was wearing himself out swinging the weight. So two men held the porker with ropes around his neck, and Grandpa confidently raised his weapon. The pig must have known what was coming, because he was determined to stare his antagonist down.

Rev. Hurd wasn't so sure of himself as he delivered his blow, and with good reason. His aim was faulty and his swing was weak, resulting in an enraged giant boar that didn't take too kindly to an unprovoked attack. He reacted instantaneously, and as you might suspect. With a maddening squeal he lunged at his attacker, who fell backward into the pigs' mudhole. The reverend squirmed through the muck on all fours, with the hog pushing him along with its snout. The only thing that saved Grandpa Hurd was the restraint the two men put on the pig as it was dragging them through the sludge. Unfortunately, halfway through they lost their grips on the ropes, so it was every man for himself.

It was evident that Rev. Hurd would never reach the fence in time, and we feared that he would be another pearl trampled underfoot. Grandpa had only one chance, and he took it. Closer than the fence was a scraggy elm tree, and he scrambled for it with moves he hadn't shown in years. No running back ever worked his way through a field of tacklers with any more art than this old man showed in dodging every thrust of his pursuer. There was just one thing wrong. The lowest limb on that tree was at least eight feet off the ground, and the reverend stood about five inches over five feet with his shoes on, which he didn't have at the time. He had no choice, however, so he was determined to try for the limb. So he jumped with all his might. But he missed! However, he caught it on the way down.

They got Grandpa out of the tree after somebody took a shotgun to his tormentor, but he didn't help with the hog killing any more that day. After his ordeal he just sat in a rocking chair on the porch. The rest of the day people would burst out laughing every time they looked at the reverend. Folks said it was the most enjoyable hog-killing day they had ever known.

Reflecting on my childhood, I can't think of a thing I would change, but I can think of a lot of things I would like to change about modern-day attitudes. It seems to me that society in general fails to assume responsibility for its own actions, tending to shift the guilt somewhere else. Criminals are not to blame for their own actions— look for the cause in their deprived childhood. This person was without a father as a role model; another was raised in poverty; another didn't have a proper environment; and on it goes. People can always find an excuse for failure, placing the blame anywhere and everywhere except where it belongs.

We were poor, but we didn't know it. We possessed the basic necessities of life and an abundance of love that provided the atmosphere in which we learned the lessons of life taught by Granny and Mama. We never allowed poverty to become a curse to us, because Granny kept burning brightly the flame of hope in our hearts. Furthermore, she did not limit the promises of God concerning better times just to life in Heaven. Those blessings were not to be postponed until the life to come; we needed them and could experience them in the life that now is. As Granny stated, "It be good to sing 'bout the Sweet By and By, but we live in the Nasty Now and Now." And she was determined that we would live it to the fullest.

Every child needs a mentor, and it rips my heart to witness the shameful neglect of children whose potential may never be realized because no one is interested or compassionate enough to take the time to guide and encourage them in their development. Javetta Saunders and I expressed this concern by collaborating on a song entitled "We Are the Children." It's available on a beautifully gripping video entitled *A Nation Under God*, in which Javetta's talented daughter, Rachel, and a group of the most adorable children you'll ever see join me in singing.

Chorus

We are the children, the children of the world
Won't you reach out your hand to some boy or some girl.
Guard and protect us, from neglect and abuse
We are the children, the future generation.

Verse 1

Here we are all alone,
We have a mother and a father but neither one is at home.
It hurts so bad, when we ask them not to go
And they pay us no mind and just walk out the door.

Verse 2

Please don't let us down, we need your wisdom
Give us a little more time; help us to get it together
Pray to the Lord above, to keep us strong
Pray for our mother and our father to make our house a home.

CHAPTER THREE

LEARNING LIFE'S LESSONS

Most people say that experience is the best teacher. I would agree with that proverb as long as we include the experience of others as well as our own. There are a lot of things I haven't experienced and don't want to, but I have learned from those who have endured them. For example, I have never known the bondage of slavery that my grandmother knew, but the wisdom she taught me enabled me to deal with the oppression born of prejudice. Granny never attended a day of school, but she taught me lessons that no textbook includes. With the addition of my mother's teachings, I must surely have a master's degree in common sense and a doctorate in practical living.

The subject areas covered in the education provided by these two instructors were respect, appreciation, and discipline. What I learned from them made me what I am today, and whatever success I have achieved I owe primarily to them.

Both Granny and Mama had graphic ways to illustrate the values they were instilling in us. They taught us with words and by personal example, to be sure, but the pictures they used were so vivid that we could never forget their object. I think they learned this method, consciously or unconsciously, from the master teacher, Jesus Christ. The favorite style of teaching that He used was telling a parable, a story based on a common everyday happening. People could actually visualize the most profound truth portrayed in unforgettable fashion. How can I ever forget Granny's lesson on a positive attitude, using a rose bush as an example!

The houses in which we lived over the years may have been simple ramshackle structures, but Granny and Mama always brightened the places with an array of flowers. On one occasion, as I was helping Granny gather rose stems, I suffered a painful thorn prick on my finger. When my crying finally subsided to sobs, I questioned the reason for thorns, vowing never again to pick a rose. As usual, Granny used the situation to teach me a lesson. "Now you listen to me, chile. 'Stead of complainin' that roses got thorns, be glad that thorns got roses." She went on to drive home to me that we could choose to major on the negative side of things or the positive side. Her choice was to view every difficulty as an opportunity, whereas other people saw difficulties in every opportunity. She had a simple, but practical and effective philosophical outlook regarding challenges and uncertainties. "Well, that be just another river to cross," she would say. She crossed a lot of them, without the benefit of bridges or sleek ferries.

I never knew Granny to look at any side but the sunny side. She thought only of the best; she worked only for the best; and she expected only the best. "Ain't nothin' worthwhile ever come easy," she declared. "I don't know of nobody ever got honey without dealin' with the bees." I knew exactly what she was talking about. When we went out to gather wild honey, we had to do battle with swarms of enraged insects that weren't going to sit by idly while we scooped up their treasure. But the reward was worth the trouble. After all, you've got to put up with the rain if you're going to enjoy the beauties of the rainbow.

Granny could tolerate failure after an honest attempt, but she had no use for someone who never tried anything for fear of failure. She stressed that anybody who takes the attitude, "I can't do it," will never accomplish very much. But the person who says, "I'll try," is capable of doing wonderful things. One time when I was playing outside Granny called me over to where she sat snapping green beans. She pointed out to me a lone ant valiantly laboring at pushing, pulling, and carrying a morsel that looked to be five times its size. She explained how diligent ants are, and how this one was striving to take food back to its colony. I asked how he was going to get to where he was going, for obviously it was a long way for an ant, especially with the burden he was carrying. She responded by telling me he was going to walk, and then she asked me if I knew the most important step the ant would take in the entire journey. I figured it would be the last one, when he finally succeeded in his task, but that was the wrong answer. "It be the first step," Granny informed me, " 'cause if he don't never take that one he ain't goin' nowhere." Somehow that makes more sense to me today than it did then, because it appears to me that there are multitudes of people with ideas, but very few who are daring enough to put them into action.

Over and over Granny told me the story of the 12 spies that Moses sent into Canaan, as recorded in Numbers 13. All the spies gave the same description of the abundance of the land, and the consensus was that the land was inhabited by fierce people so large that the Israelites looked like grasshoppers in comparison. Ten of the spies concluded that it would be impossible to conquer the land against such odds. However, two of them, Joshua and Caleb, disagreed, arguing that the Israelites should march into the land immediately. After all, if God had already given the land to them, then surely He would enable them to overcome all enemies, no matter how strong they were. Unfortunately, the people chose to receive the bad report, and they were doomed to wander in the wilderness for the next 38 years before entering Canaan and fulfilling the purpose and will of God for them. Of all the adults among the two million or so, Joshua and Caleb were the only ones who survived to enter the land.

Granny's point was that those who don't try because of fear of failure will never succeed at anything. She went on to explain that 45 years later, when Joshua was dividing the land among the tribes of Israel, Caleb, now 85 years old, made a request. He asked to be given the most difficult part of the country to conquer, still occupied by the giants, because he was confident that the Lord would enable him to drive them out (see Josh. 14:8-13). According to Granny, "the Bible say Caleb had a different spirit" (see Num. 14:24). "He don't say, 'Give me strength to match my mountain'; he say, 'Give me a mountain to match my strength.' " She taught me by way of application that my first question about anything should not be "Is it possible?" I should ask instead, "Is it right?" or "Is it what God wants?" She explained that if I did only what I thought possible in my own ability,

I would put a limit on what God could do through me. She firmly believed that "God make the impossible possible." She encouraged me always to follow the Lord, wherever He leads. "When Jesus told the disciples, 'Follow Me,' " she pointed out, "They don't ask, 'Where we goin'?' "

She urged me to be of "a different spirit" than those who say, "It can't be done." From the time I was old enough to understand, she drilled into me the certainty that I could be an achiever, and at the same time she instilled in me a sense of dignity. "Ain't nobody can make you feel like you are worthless lessen you agree with them," she told me. Because of her encouragement, I grew up believing that I could really do and be something, and that circumstances could not hold me back.

Granny's teaching also served me well in later life as I struggled with career decisions. She taught me to pray about such things, and then to act on what I felt to be God's will, not worrying that it might be wrong. "Anybody worry about goin' wrong won't never go right neither," was the way she put it. She impressed upon me that the important thing was to have a heart to obey. Then if I missed God's way, He would correct me. But I would never know how far I could go with God unless I took the risk of going too far. "The Bible say whether you turn left or right, your ears goin' hear God's voice behind you telling you, 'This be the way; walk in it' " (see Is. 30:21). Countless times I have relied upon that bit of wisdom, and I have acted upon it.

Both Granny and Mama taught me to work hard, stressing that people have a greater appreciation for what they earn. "Nobody owe you nothin' 'cept what you work for," was their credo. And once I agreed to do a job, I was honor bound to do my best, and not to take shortcuts. "Even if the boss-man ain't lookin', the Lord got His eye on you. You always do your work for the Lord, you always goin' do a good job." I try to live by that guidance to this very day. If I agree to do a concert, I will strive to perform at the same level, regardless of the size and makeup of the audience. I always interact with the crowd, but ultimately my aim is to please Jesus and to glorify Him. He gave His all for me, holding nothing back, and I can do no less for Him.

The work ethic I practice today began as a child with the discipline drilled into me by my two mentors. From their wisdom I learned the practice of diligence in accomplishing any task, and that anything worth doing is worth doing well. There were a lot of times that I did a second-rate job, and I always had an explanation for the poor performance. However, Granny wouldn't tolerate any of it. "Boy, you used more time 'splaining to me why you done it wrong than it would have taken to do it right." With that kind of analysis, do you wonder why I could never get by with anything?

As a matter of fact, Granny and Mama would never allow me to settle for less than my best effort in anything. One time when I slacked off in the cotton field, Mama got on my case. My defense was that I had picked as much as my buddy James. Mama's nostrils flared and for a moment I thought she was going to whack me. But with a sigh she said, "Listen, boy, at the end of the day's work you don't measure what you done by what somebody else done. You measure it by what you should have done and could have done. James ain't your standard; the best you can do is your standard."

That principle has been the basis of my self-evaluation over the years. Doing as good as or better than someone else is not enough. The only acceptable comparison is to compare what I am with what I ought to be and could be and what I have done with what I should have done and could have done. Only as I measure up fully to that standard can I feel satisfaction in my person and in my performance.

A kindred principle I learned in my pre-teen years was that I can't make myself bigger by making others appear smaller. To state it another way, I can't advance myself by pushing others down. I came home from school one day gloating over the quality of my performance, while belittling and criticizing the efforts of a classmate. I got a blast from both barrels, one called Granny and the other called Mama. Granny fired first: "Bish, you spend as much time as you ought to tryin' to get better yourself, you ain't goin' have no time to criticize nobody else." (As a child everyone called me after my middle name, Bishop.) Then Mama took aim and hit the target: "Bish, as long as you put somebody down you ain't goin' nowhere, 'cause you got to stay down there with him to hold him down. That mean you can't get where you could go."

Simple words, but profound truth! And whenever I am tempted to elevate myself at someone else's expense, I can still feel the impact of the verbal blasts from Granny and Mama.

One of my favorite lessons was the one Granny taught us about the "Tater" family. She could always make work seem more like play by entertaining us in various ways. When we dug potatoes she would sometimes give names to odd-shaped ones, and naturally a story accompanied each one. On one particular potato-digging day she put aside several choice spuds, explaining that they were the "Tater" family.

The first member of the family was "Imitator." "All he know to do is copy what other folks doing. He don't never do nothin' his very own." Then there was "Spectator." "He always watchin' what other folks doin', but he too lazy to do anything hisself." Another one was "Commentator," who "so busy talkin' about what other folks doin', ain't got time to do nothin' else." Also among the group was "Agitator," who "don't do nothin' but stir up trouble." The best of all was "Meditator," who could be good or bad, depending on what he was thinking about. "Y'all be careful what y'all think about," Granny said, " 'cause the Book say as y'all think, that what y'all goin' be." She went on to teach us the process by which thoughts are translated into character. Thoughts become words; words become actions; actions become habits; habits become character.

Some lessons I learned were underscored by rather demonstrative means. Contrary to the impression I may give today, I wasn't always angelic in my behavior as a youth. For example, one day I was somewhat forceful in stressing a point to my sister June. She ran screaming to Mama that I had pulled her hair, spat on her, and called her a bad name. Most people gauge their mother's mood by the tone of her voice. I did that too, but I had another indication that gave a more accurate reading. Whenever Mama used my full name, I knew I was in trouble. This time all alarm signals were blaring when Mama hollered in a voice that I figured could be heard in the next county: "Charles Bishop Johnson, you get yourself here right this minute!" Assuming my most cherubic appearance, I meekly approached with questioning innocence: "Did you call me, Mama?" My pretense didn't work. There stood June, still sobbing within the fold of Mama's protective arm, and I was discomfited, though not surprised, to see a long limber willow switch in Mama's free hand. "Boy, you better tell me the truth, and if you don't it's going to be twice as hard on you. Did you pull your sister's hair, spit on her, and call her a bad name?"

I honestly don't know why she asked, when she already knew the answer to her question. I knew there wasn't a chance to squirm out of the situation, so I assumed the most contrite appearance I could, down to the quivering bottom lip and the catch in my voice, and admitted my guilt. "The devil done made you do that," Mama declared. To which I responded, "Well, the devil made me pull her hair and call her a bad name, but spitting on her was my idea."

Actually, all of it was my idea, but I thought perhaps I would receive two-thirds less punishment if I acknowledged one-third of the responsibility. My ploy not only failed to work, but it also achieved the opposite effect. Quicker than a striking rattler, Mama's arm shot out and in one motion my wrist was gripped in the steely grasp of her hand, while my backside was positioned at the proper striking distance. If you have never felt the whip-like sting of a supple willow switch about four feet long, you have missed an unforgettable experience, but I wouldn't advise you to try it just for the sake of adventure. As Mama was lashing me she was saying, "I'll teach you to respect your sister!" Believe me, she was an excellent teacher, and at that moment I was a very attentive student. So well did I learn the lesson Mama was teaching, I have not only maintained the utmost respect for my sister ever since, but I went beyond the lesson plan to learn deep respect for all womanhood.

Now I know that corporal punishment of children isn't so acceptable today, and is in fact illegal in some places. I read in the newspaper about a woman who gave a well-deserved smack on the bottom to her misbehaving child in a supermarket. Unknown to her, a busybody who had witnessed the incident followed the woman as she and her child left the store. She wrote down the license number of the lady's car and proceeded to call the authorities and report her for child abuse. That afternoon strong-armed representatives from the state's social services department arrived without warning. They took the screaming child to a foster home and the bewildered and protesting mother to the police station, where she was photographed, fingerprinted, and subjected to psychiatric tests and a thorough investigation of her personal life, including embarrassing interviews with neighbors, employers, and others. All of this because she administered proper correction to her child!

When I was in school the teacher's accessories included the usual assortment of pencils, erasers, chalk, and the like, just as you can typically find today. However, one item that was a fixture on the teacher's desk is conspicuously missing from the modern classroom. As common to a teacher as a blackboard eraser was a wooden paddle at least four inches wide and three feet long, sometimes with a hole in the business part of it for greater effect. I can give vivid personal testimony to the fact that she used the paddle quite frequently, and at her own discretion. One time I knew I was due a paddling because of my misconduct on the playground, so I decided to prepare for the inevitable. I put the largest book I had, which happened to be a geography text, in the seat of my overalls. I felt no pain at all as Mrs. Reese whacked me. By the third blow, she figured that something was amiss because of the lack of reaction on my part. When she found out that she had been pounding Outer Mongolia instead of Lower Charles, she gave me a double portion.

I never resented any of my teachers for the discipline they administered; rather, I considered it part of the educational process that taught respect for authority and the rights of others. A society that treats wrongdoers more like victims, such as we have today, encourages the attitude of "what's in it for me?" As a result of this godless self-centeredness, we have a disobedient, ungrateful, disrespectful generation, together with the absence of restraint, loyalty, prudence, and humility. God's order, as plainly declared in Scripture, is that we love Him first (with all our heart, soul, mind, and strength), our neighbor next, and our self last. If we reverse the order of the first and third, putting self first and God last, our neighbor in the middle is bound to suffer.

Both by personal example and biblical teaching, Granny and Mama led me to develop an attitude that seeks to serve the other person rather than self. Somehow Granny learned about the Dead Sea. By simply studying a map of the Holy Land in her Bible, she explained why nothing can live in that particular body of water. She saw that the Jordan River flows into it, but noticed that there is no outflow. "That the problem," she reflected. "It always takin' in, but don't ever give out. You always receive but don't give, you goin' have no life and you goin' stagnate."

I can remember my mother constantly singing the song, "It's My Desire to Help Someone Along the Way," as she did her chores, and that's exactly how she lived. One bright fall day she called my attention to a flock of geese flying directly overhead in a perfect "V" formation. As we watched, the lead goose at the point of the formation dropped back to the rear and another one moved up to take the position. Mama explained that the geese at the front of the formation

Mama

made it easier for the others to follow, and that they could fly much farther by rotating positions when they tired. This visual lesson was an impressionable way to teach me the value of helping one another, and that in giving we also receive.

Granny and Mama practiced what they preached. As I think back I can remember a lifetime of specific acts of self-giving on their part. Countless times there didn't appear to be any reward for their service, but they cheerfully went about their business with the confidence that their deeds had not gone unnoticed by the Lord. I have tried to follow their example by helping others, regardless of whether or not they could do anything for me. I have heard preachers say that love in the New Testament means to put the other person above yourself and to seek his highest good even at your own expense. That principle is the direct opposite of the modern attitude of "me first." After Paul appealed to us to forego our own interests for the sake of others, he enforced his exhortation by pointing to Jesus, who left the royalties of Heaven to come to earth as a man and die for us (see Phil. 2:4-8). Shouldn't we have the same kind of servant attitude?

When it came to teaching lessons in morality, Granny and Mama would sometimes resort to forcible means. Burned into my memory forever is my first sight of the scars my grandmother wore as an insignia of her enslavement. She was trying to impress upon us the consequences of wrongdoing and the blessings of right living. I can never forget the horror that gripped me when she slipped her dress from around her shoulders and allowed us to view her back. Her skin was crisscrossed with knotty ropes of ugly scar tissue that looked like a relief map of the Great Smoky Mountains. "This what happen when you don't do right," she explained. "Be good and you don't get beat." It amazes me as I reflect on her attitude that she could assume responsibility for the scars on her body, as though she deserved them. I could never imagine my grandmother guilty of any crime, but her heart was so full of forgiveness and so void of bitterness and resentment that she could defend those who had grievously wronged her. At any rate, her demonstration was an effective deterrent in keeping me from gross misconduct.

Mama also contributed to the fear of punishment ingrained in me by Granny's dramatic object lesson. When I was about six years old she took me to the jail in Paris, having prepared me for the visit by telling me what happens when people do bad things. At the jail I was ushered into the presence of the biggest, most menacing-looking man I had ever seen. The flashy badge that to me appeared to cover half his chest was convincing evidence of his authority, but the cannon-like gun strapped to his waist left no doubt that he was in charge. And if Samson could slay a thousand Philistines with the jawbone of a donkey, I knew this giant officer could have done at least half as well with the polished club hanging from his belt. The scowl on his stern unsmiling face spoke far more to me than a hundred lectures could have. I was literally trembling as he gave me a harsh admonition to obey my mother and to do right. At that moment if he had told me to jump I would have asked how high on the way up. I didn't realize until much later that Mama had arranged that little interview. People might question her method, but it proved effective in my case, since I have always maintained a healthy respect for authority, even when I disagreed with it.

I suffered inexpressible misery the only time I can remember defying the values Granny and Mama molded into my character. One day when I was 12 years old a kind white lady gave me some money to buy some candy. Instead, I bought a plug of Brown Mule chewing tobacco. Why they called it that I'll never understand, because any mule has better sense than to chew the foul stuff. Anyway, a few days earlier my buddy Lester had surprised me by biting off a chaw from a plug he took from his pocket. Wide-eyed, I asked, "Lester, do you mean to tell me that you chew tobacco?" Spewing out a stream of the brown liquid just as professionally as the loafers in front of the store, he wiped his mouth with the back of his hand and responded, "Yeah, and I cusses too!" Well, I was too respectful or scared of the Lord and Granny to cuss, but the temptation to prove my manhood by actually taking a chaw of tobacco was irresistible.

Whatever stimulating effect chewing tobacco is supposed to have, I received the full effect as the tocsin sounded every alarm in my system. My brain was the first to react, stupefied to the extent that the signals it sent to my body were so confusing that I was completely disoriented, reeling in all directions until I hit the ground. It was the only time in my life that I have been drunk. My stomach quickly became a participant in the wretchedness. I don't know what color a mixture of green and black makes, but whatever it is, I was it. The only rational thought I had was Granny's pronouncement concerning the fact that the wages of sin is death. Right then I felt that I was going to be a prime example of that truth. Adding to my indignity was the realization that the soft squishy stuff underneath my body where I had fallen was a freshly deposited cow pie. I didn't even have the equilibrium to roll out of the manure. I finally regained my balance, but the worse was yet to come. I looked and stank like something the hogs rejected, and Mama wouldn't let me in the house until I stripped and washed at the pump. When I explained to her, half-truthfully, that sickness had caused me to fall where I did, I discovered that in this particular instance the wages of sin was not death, but a generous dose of the inevitable castor oil.

No Timothy ever had a better Lois or Eunice to teach him than I had. Everything worthwhile that I know I learned from my grandmother and my mother, and I am forever indebted to them.

CHAPTER FOUR

SETTING GOD'S POETRY IN MOTION

Ephesians 2:10 declares that we are God's "workmanship, created in Christ Jesus for good works, which God prepared beforehand that we should walk in them." I have been told that the Greek word translated "workmanship" is the word from which the English word *poem* comes. I am God's poem, His work of art. Without Him my life has no rhyme or reason. Only He brings order, balance, and harmony. As the Master Designer, God prepared a way in which I should walk, and He appointed and equipped me to walk in it.

In retrospect, it's evident that God wrote the poem that would be my life long before I was born. The unfolding of the course He had charted for me began when I was only a toddler. With Mama's six sisters and three brothers, you can well imagine that I was surrounded by a passel of cousins, unnumbered to this very day. A common feature at every family gathering was gospel singing, and in time smaller musical groups evolved out of the larger crowd. One such group of my older cousins, who called themselves The Harmony

Kings, began to sing regularly in area churches. I'm told that as a two-year-old child I was enthralled by their music to the point that I would listen to them rehearsing and performing for hours, clapping and dancing as they sang. As I grew older I never tired of listening to them, attending their rehearsal sessions, and begging to accompany them when they went to different churches. Rhythm became so natural to me that I thought with it and moved with it, and I looked forward to the day when I would be old enough to join the group.

In the first years of my life we moved constantly from one place to another, around the same general area, but in no place did we have plumbing or electricity. However, when I was about five years old Mama managed to get a small, cheap, battery-operated radio, which we listened to every night, and a whole new world was revealed to me. Of course, we tuned in to the usual mysteries, comedies, dramas, and variety programs, but our favorites were the music programs, particularly those featuring gospel music. WMS out of Nashville was our mainstay, and the Grand Ole Opry was as much a part of our family as churchgoing on Sunday. I knew Minnie Pearl, Roy Acuff, Ernest Tubb, Red Foley, Grandpa Jones, and other Opry singers better than many of my cousins. In addition, I could sing right along with The Fairfield Four, The Chuck Wagon Gang, and especially with my favorites, Bill and Joe Callahan. The music went far past my physical hearing. It found a lodging place in my very soul and became part of my existence. Soon, music would become even more of a passion, but not before I had an unforgettable experience that would prove to be a strong influence in my life.

Decades later the memory is as vivid and fresh as though the event occurred only yesterday. It happened one sunny day in the summer of my seventh year. I was playing with an old tire, rolling it down the dirt road that passed our house. There was nothing particularly different that set that occasion apart from any other habitual playtime. Yet, I suppose the ordinariness of the scene was what made the incident stand out in greater contrast. Words are painfully inadequate to express what I saw and felt, so the most I can do is to try to give an objective description without communicating the overpowering feeling that came over me.

As I raced along with the rolling tire in the shade of an arbor formed by the overhanging branches of trees on opposite sides of the lane, I became conscious of an unusual stillness and quietness. There was a profound sense of peace all around, which not even the rustling of a leaf or the buzzing of an insect or the chirp of a bird dared to disturb. The place seemed hallowed by a divine presence. Suddenly, an unearthly stream of light shot from the sky like an arrow aimed directly at me. I looked around the spot where I was standing and found that while everything else was in shadow, I was engulfed in a single shaft of sunlight that pierced the foliage overhead. The trees might as well have had no leaves at all, for the dazzling stream of light flowed unhindered. The brightness that surrounded me seemed to be many times stronger than ordinary rays of sunshine, more like the intensity of a white-heat glow. It was as though the eye of the sun had singled me out and concentrated the energy of a thousand scattered beams of light into one, which it focused on me. At that time I had never seen an airport, but since then I have likened it to the strength of a powerful beacon piercing the darkness. The warmth that I felt was not from the heat of the sun. Rather than originating from an outward physical factor, it arose from within me and suffused my entire being. It was something like warm oil flowing over my body. I heard no sound as I stood transfixed to the spot, but I knew that a divine presence was with me and that some kind of anointing had come upon me. It must have been with me as it was with the people of God in Isaiah's time: "Arise, shine; for your light has come! And the glory of the Lord is risen upon you" (Is. 60:1).

Although I was only a child, I somehow knew that my destiny was shaped and that I would pursue a purpose. I have never escaped the reality of that experience, and it has recurred in dreams on many occasions. At the time I certainly did not have full understanding of the significance of what had happened. It was only later that it began to unfold, when I learned Proverbs 3:5-6 in Sunday school: "Trust in the Lord with all your heart, and lean not on your own understanding; in all your ways acknowledge Him, and He shall direct your paths." I was convinced that this was God's way of assuring me of something that He was doing in my life, and from that time I knew I would travel the world and sing of God's glory.

Does a seven-year-old child dare to share such a personal and weighty occurrence for fear of scornful dismissal? I pondered the matter for a long time before concluding that this was something from the Lord meant only for me. As much as I knew that Granny would understand and that she would offer wise and gentle counsel, I carefully guarded the vision I had been granted. However, I could not contain my curiosity about the way to accomplish what God wanted me to do. A year or so after my experience, I approached Granny with the question that had occupied me. "You got to do two things," she answered. "You got to pray and you got to work. Some people is all work without prayer, and all they doin' is trustin' in their own strength. The only time some people pray is when they want to get somethin' or get out of somethin', but that ain't the way. But while you prayin', you got to work. Some folks are good people, but good for nothin'. God don't want us to be so heavenly minded we no earthly good, and He don't want us to go walkin' around with our heads so high in the clouds our feet don't touch the ground."

To illustrate her point, she told me a story about Liza, a domestic slave on a neighboring plantation. Liza's mistress was a godly woman who was quite concerned about a notorious roadhouse in the area, where all kinds of unholy pursuits were carried out. So the lady enlisted Liza's help in praying that the Lord would remove such a den of iniquity. The next day she was quite excited to learn that during the night the place had burned completely to the ground. She shared the news with Liza, along with a question. "How is it," she wondered, "that I have prayed fervently for months, and nothing happened; then you prayed only one day and your prayer was answered immediately?" "Well, ma'am," Liza coyly replied, "sometimes the Lord expects us to put feet to our prayers!"

Whether the story was a fact or a fable, it impressed me to the realization that while we must be diligent in prayer, we also must be active in pursuing the object of our prayers. That understanding became even clearer to me when Granny taught me one of her living parables. She asked me if I thought I could climb a wobbly home-made ladder leaning against the house. To a country boy like me, such a question as that was an insult, and I rushed over to show Granny how fast I could scoot up the ladder. "Just a minute," she called. "I want you to do your climbing with your hands in your pockets." Now that seemed rather foolish to me, but I did as she instructed. I managed the first couple of rungs fairly easily, but the higher I climbed the less steady and secure I became. I could go no further. Then she told me to finish the climb, using my hands. This I quickly did and then descended. "Now, Bish, tell me what you learned." Well, I didn't have a clue as to what Granny wanted me to say, so I just responded with the obvious: "I can't climb a ladder with my hands in my pockets." What was her point? "Ain't nobody goin' climb to where God wants him to go with his hands in his pockets." That was her way of teaching me that while everybody wants to succeed, few are willing to pay the price.

I may have learned the rewards of practice too well, especially when I had saved enough money from picking cotton to buy a little record player and some gospel records. By the time I was about eleven years old, power lines had reached the area where we lived, and that record player was the first electrical device we ever had in our house. I played those records repeatedly day and night until they were so scratched the music sounded more like the frantic screeching of a long-tailed cat trying to find its way out of a roomful of rocking chairs. I knew the words and the tunes to all the songs, such as "The Milky White Way" by The Trumpeteers, "I'm Working on a Building" by The Swan Silvertones, "Jesus, You're My Water" by The Soul Stirrers, and "God Said He Would Send Down the Fire" by the Dixieaires. The problem was that everybody else knew that I knew the songs. It was a three-mile walk to school and the same distance coming home, and I was singing every step of the way. Pretty soon I noticed that I was walking by myself most of the way. I couldn't restrain myself; I sang more than I talked. I sang at play; I sang in the cotton fields; I sang when I had to visit the outhouse; I sang to the chickens, the horses, and the pigs.

It was providential that I had those records, because from them I learned the art of writing lyrics. The message expressed in those songs came straight from the Bible, and I have tried to follow the same pattern in every song I have written. Through the years individuals and recording agencies have offered me lucrative deals to sing their kind of music, especially rock. I admit that the financial rewards were tempting, but I never had a desire to sing anything but gospel. To be truthful, I barely listen to secular music, because it has no appeal to me. I was born to sing, to be sure, but within certain limitations.

I didn't have a voice teacher or an opportunity to take music lessons, but I did have a shorthaired mongrel dog named Brownie, who would protect me with his life. Now what I'm about to tell may seem crazy, but it makes sense to me. Every time I started singing, Brownie would sit on his haunches, lift his head, and start howling. When I stopped, he stopped. I don't know whether he was complaining or joining in the concert, but I declare that it had an effect on me. In the midst of all that racket, I learned how to concentrate without being distracted and drawn off key. Brownie was the closest thing to a music professor I had in those formative years, and I owe a debt of gratitude to him.

The days of my boyhood were before the giant strides of the civil rights movement, and opportunities that we take for granted now were rare at that time. Where I lived most people witnessed the same cycle of life repeated over and over. They knew their place and occupied it, eking out a bare existence, working in the fields, marrying and breeding children, and dying in the same conditions in which they were born. Not many escaped that cycle, and most didn't even talk about it. However, I had inherited enough of my grandmother's spirit and received enough of her teachings to think otherwise. I can't honestly say that at that time of my life I was fully aware of being motivated by divine power, but later it became apparent beyond all doubt.

No one in those formative years sought to stifle my interest in music, and I suffered no ridicule when I talked about becoming a singer. On the other hand, I received very little encouragement. At best, most people simply tolerated me. Only my mother and grandmother understood my desire and expressed belief in me. Granny even referred to me as her "star," and she wasn't just humoring me. I always felt older and wiser than my years when she and Mama built me up, and I was always strengthened in my resolve to be a gospel singer.

I truly believe that more people fall short of their potential because of lack of encouragement than for any other reason. Although I had a burning passion within me to be a singer, I don't know how it would have been realized without the support of those close to me. I believe that adults, especially parents and other relatives, should take time to discover and share children's interests and talents and dreams, making every effort to help them develop those pursuits. It's heartbreaking to see children falling by the wayside because of indifference or unkind put-downs by their elders. When I read statistics concerning crime, violence, drugs, and other problems among the youth of our land, especially in the crowded ghettos, I wonder how many lives could be different if someone had taken a little time and effort to give encouragement and support. How many books and songs have never been written, how many masterpieces have never been painted, and how many other potentials have been unrealized because of someone's neglect? I'm certain that there are a great many talented and gifted people who never fulfill all that God has planned for them. And the tragic truth is that most times it isn't lack of knowledge or desire that holds them back; more often the explanation is that no one has bothered to pat them on the back and cheer them on, or at least speak an encouraging word. Solomon expressed it very well: "Hope deferred makes the heart sick, but when the desire comes, it is a tree of life," and "A word spoken in due season, how good it is!" (Prov. 13:12; 15:23)

CHAPTER FIVE

WORKING OUT WHAT GOD WORKS IN

My hour had finally come! This was the moment for which I had prepared, for which I had dreamed, for which I had prayed, for which I had begged and schemed. The momentous occasion was my debut as part of a gospel singing group, actually performing before a live audience. The group was The Harmony Kings, composed of four of my older cousins. Since I was two years old I had been listening to them rehearse for hours at a time, and I had attended every one of their performances to which I could wheedle a ride. I knew every song in their repertoire, and even more because of my record collection. It was to shut me up that they gave me this opportunity. I was now in the summer of my fifteenth year, and I had been pestering them mercilessly for at least the last ten years to include me in their group. My dogged persistence finally wore them down, and here I was about to sing the lead as we belted out "The Milky White Way."

I have to admit that I didn't quite fit the image of a Harmony King. They were older by many years, with voices trained by experience and mellowed by maturity. I was a gangling youngster whose voice was still in transition between childhood and manhood. They were dressed in their snazzy identical gabardine blue suits, white shirts, and red and blue striped ties. I didn't own anything that resembled a suit, and what I finally wound up with after scrounging an assortment of clothing from various cousins and uncles sort of set me apart from the others. I was wearing a black fuzzy wool jacket mismatched with slick trousers whose color could best be described as aqua-lavender. Both the coat and the trousers were several sizes too big for me and kind of swallowed me. I didn't have a belt, but a pair of enormous red suspenders held up my oversized pants. My shirt was lemon yellow and my tie was a survivor of the depression years, at least eight inches wide with green, red, and purple floral patterns against a pink background. Uncle Lish had discovered it at the bottom of an old trunk after he recalled having won it at a county fair about ten years earlier. We probably didn't know how to tie it, because it seemed to be a little long, ending at least six inches below my waist. The Kings were wearing two-toned black and white oxfords, so shiny spit-polished that you could see your reflection in them. I was shod in my brown Sears-Roebuck brogans, scuffed with hard wear. That was okay, because nobody could see them anyway, with the cuffs of my elongated pants completely covering them and dragging along the floor.

Thinking back on the scene, I wonder if I didn't look as out of place as a white-sheeted Ku Klux Klansman at a NAACP convention. It must not have been all that bad, because nobody made any comment, much less snicker. I couldn't help but notice though, that Cousin Ezell, the head King, was sweating more than usual as he cast uneasy looks at me, and it wasn't all due to the stifling heat of the June afternoon. Me, I was oblivious to my appearance and the heat. I might as well have been clad in a classy tuxedo, ready to sing in the air-conditioned comfort of a plush concert hall before a thousand or more people. This little country church near Paris, Texas, crammed with a congregation of 150 or so, was glory to me. I felt nothing of the oppressive heat and I was totally unaffected by the anxieties of the Kings. I had paid the price and now I was ready to reap the reward.

In retrospect, I guess the Kings were a little nervous about me, having second thoughts about letting me sing with them even for just one song. After all, they had a reputation to protect. Never mind my appearance; it was my singing that concerned them. They really didn't think I had it in me, but probably felt they could drown me out and cover for me.

Before I sang, I couldn't help but close my eyes and reminisce for a few moments, which brought the added benefit of having people think I was in meditative prayer. I know the Kings were doing some real praying! Only four brief years had passed since I had bought my little record player, but they were years of stern discipline that had shaped my future. During that time we lived and worked on a farm owned by a white man by the name of Grover Donnell. While I continued to work in the field, Mr. Donnell, having discovered my interest in animals, gave me the opportunity to work with the mules, horses, and cows. It soon became apparent that even though I wasn't yet in my teens I had a special aptitude when it came to animals, and I was entrusted with a lot of responsibility. Mr. Donnell owned two sale barns, and on sale days my job was to sort the animals according to their owners. Most days I would tag as many as 3,500 horses and cattle. I learned a great deal about animals and soon developed an expertise in working with them. I didn't know it at the time, but I was also gaining a reputation for dependability and skill in handling stock. Of course I sang constantly to the animals, and I think they responded to me either because I kept them entertained or frightened. Regardless of the explanation, the good reports I received were soon to play a major role in the direction of my life.

In addition to my passion for singing, I nurtured the dream of playing the guitar. I was captivated not only by the lyrics and melodies of the songs I heard, but by the rhythmical twang of strings plucked with such mastery that the instrument seemed miraculously to possess a voice of its own. For hours at rehearsals and performances I studied deft fingers skipping up and down and across strings, fascinated by the sounds they produced. Then when I was alone I would pick up a board or a stick and mimic what I had seen, pretending to accompany myself as I was singing. But I had no guitar, and there was no one to teach me even if I did have one. That didn't stop me from watching and wanting, though.

I finally found a benefactor when I was about fourteen years old. I was still working on the Donnell farm. Both Mr. Donnell and his wife Lelia showed a great deal of kindness to me, especially Mrs. Donnell. One day she learned about a used guitar that could be bought for four dollars. Without telling me why she was doing it, she pressed four crumpled dollar bills into my hand and told me to buy that guitar. That's exactly what I did, ignoring the fact that all I knew about playing it was how to hold it. In Heaven I want to tell Mrs.

Donnell what dividends her four-dollar investment brought. It took a long time, and a lot of persistence and discipline, but without a teacher or lessons I learned to play the guitar. I haven't looked back since, and I have never regretted one moment I devoted to practice. It seems to me that a lot of folks nowadays want things to come easy, handed to them on a silver platter. They say they want something, but they don't want it badly enough to pay the price. Not much ever came easy for me, but I had enough of my grandmother's teachings in me to stay the course and work hard for what I wanted. I feel something like the master violinist must have felt when someone rushed up to him after a concert and exclaimed: "I'd give my whole life to play as beautifully as you do!" The violinist replied, "I did." As far as I know the only place you find success before work is in the dictionary.

I had worked, and now here I was on the platform of the church with The Harmony Kings, nervous as a nudist about to crawl through a barbed-wire fence. But this was inauguration day, a graduation from the private conservatory I had been attending, where I was both the only student and the only instructor. This was birthday, Christmas, Independence Day, and Easter all rolled into one eventful day, and I was going to make the most of it. The song seemed to last no more than 30 seconds. I was flying in another dimension, far beyond the Milky Way we were singing about, so high I didn't know if I would ever come down. No daredevil ride at the fairgrounds could ever be this thrilling. I had found my element; my course was fixed, and nothing would ever turn me aside from that chosen path. If there had ever been any tinge of doubt that I would become a gospel singer, it was now forever smothered. I can honestly say that I have never wavered from my calling since then, even through the most difficult times that were to come.

I wish I could report that after we sang the people roared to their feet in thunderous applause, shouting my name and proclaiming me as a boy wonder that would revolutionize gospel music. In reality they were polite enough in their reception; whether out of pity or genuine appreciation, I don't know. The Kings looked relieved, and I think I detected a hint of surprise on their part that I had performed better than they thought I could. Whatever they thought at the time, they never asked me to sing with them again. As it turned out, that was for the best, because God had something else in mind.

After most people had left, one of the Kings told me that someone wanted to talk to me. The gentleman who summoned me turned out to be a tall beanpole of a man named Robert Percy. He looked to be about fifty, ancient by my standards. He was soft-spoken, and when he spoke you knew you were listening to a wise man. His characteristics were such that after a while you tended to forget the fact that he was totally blind. He was a voice teacher who taught harmony to choirs and individuals, and he evidently recognized some potential in me, because he presented me with an opportunity I couldn't refuse. Mr. Percy had taken an interest in a group that called themselves The Loving Five, made up of boys my age. He somewhat managed them, arranging engagements for them and going with them to performances. Well, it so happened that the Five were now only Four, and they needed one more singer to live up to their name. I was stunned when Mr. Percy asked if I would be interested in bringing the group up to full complement. I couldn't have reacted with more enthusiasm than if he had asked me if I wanted to make the Blackwood Brothers Quartet a quintet.

If this gracious man had known what a trial I would be to his patience during the next year, he probably would never have asked me to join The Loving Five. I spent every available minute I had at his house, soaking in all that he could teach me. When the others showed up for practice, I heard the teaching again. It was from this man that I learned the principles of harmony. Even more than applying what he taught to my singing, I learned to apply it to my listening, which made me more conscientious as a singer. In other words, I learned from Mr. Percy the ingredients that make music what it is, not only things having to do with pitch and harmony and such, but the heart and soul of music. Music is more than just words correctly sung in a certain key to a certain beat and rhythm. In order for a song to be music, it must not only have language; it must have heart. You can express far more in music than you can in words, if the music is truly birthed within you. I have heard countless singers who could deliver every note with perfection. They were coldly correct, but devoid of feeling. I guess I'm talking about an anointing to sing. Mr. Percy taught me to see and to communicate something beyond printed notes and words. To this day, when I sing I'm expressing what I feel, in the way that I feel it, so that the music is simply an audible manifestation of my inmost being.

I knew Mr. Percy for only a year, during which time he shepherded The Loving Five as a father. He booked engagements for us and went with us, always encouraging us and pointing out ways we could improve. In between engagements we practically lived at his house, so eager were we to learn. Unfortunately, he died when I was sixteen years old, but I'm a better man today because of him. You probably won't read the name of Robert Percy outside these pages, but he was one of those men whom Jesus described as great in Heaven's estimation. I'm glad I can finally pay tribute to him in some small measure.

The Loving Five was a group of teenagers, ages 14 to 16, but mature enough to be committed to a purpose. We sang anywhere and every time we had the opportunity. When we didn't have a place, we would often sing a capella on street corners. Like most boys my age in those days, I had dropped out of school; however, I did finish the tenth grade, further than many others were able to go. I regret that I didn't finish high school, and I offer no excuse except the necessities of livelihood brought on by the difficulties of that day. There is no doubt that had I stayed in school, I could have attended college on an athletic scholarship, because I had gained quite a reputation as a hard-nosed football player. I had worked ever since I could pull cotton out of a boll, steadily gaining experience in various areas of manual labor; and at the age of 16 I was carrying out a man's work at the cotton mill in Paris, but still keeping alive the dream of being a full-time gospel singer.

My life took a decided turn shortly after I began working at the cotton mill. My older cousin Ezell, of The Harmony Kings, had gone to work on a ranch near Abilene, where he heard that the rancher, Mr. Davis, was looking for someone to break his horses. When Ezell told him about me, Mr. Davis responded that I could have the job if I wanted it. So Ezell came all the way back to Paris to take me to the ranch. I had never before traveled outside the county and I can't recall ever having eaten a meal that one of my relatives had not prepared. Now at the age of 16 I was about to become a full-fledged cowboy, away from home for the first time. I may have left my mother and grandmother behind, but I could never have deserted the teachings they had poured into me. When I left Mama told me that she knew she would never have to worry about me, because no matter where I went, the hand of God would be upon me. I have always kept fresh in my mind her last admonitions before I climbed into Ezell's pickup—always to be myself, real and sincere, with nothing superficial. Her only negative plea was for me to stay away from strong drink and promiscuous women.

I couldn't have had a better role model and guardian than Ezell, who was more like an older brother to me than a cousin. That was especially true since his father, Benjamin Harrison Kendrick, who was married to Ella, my mother's sister, had always acted as a substitute father to me. Uncle Harrison was a simple sharecropper without education, but at the same time, he was a remarkable man, full of wisdom and a devout Christian. When that man prayed there was no doubt about the personal presence of the Lord. In fact, there were times in the midst of his prayers that I opened my eyes and looked around, fully expecting to see Jesus or at least some angels hovering nearby. He was a tall, strong man who never wasted time. He lived to be 99 years old, and was still driving a pickup and doing fieldwork at the time. This physical giant was the most sensitive, gentle, and caring man I have ever known, and he poured himself into my life. I never had to ask him for advice; he was always ahead of me and gave me sound counsel. Next to Mama and Granny, Uncle Harrison had the most profound influence over me during my growing-up years. So the fact that I would be under the protective care of Cousin Ezell, his son, overcame any reluctance that Mama might have had in consenting to my departure.

The next two years were a time of maturing. I was at the Davis ranch only a short while before bad health forced Mr. Davis' retirement, after which I moved on to a ranch owned by Mr. and Mrs. Green. During that time I literally reached physical, emotional, and mental manhood. Although I had few opportunities to sing publicly, my dream of a full-time career in gospel singing was as dominant as ever, and I kept busy developing my skills as I practiced before a noncritical audience of hundreds of animals. I also attended every singing event I could get to, observing, listening, and learning.

My ranching career came to an abrupt end when Mr. and Mrs. Green were both killed in a car accident while they were on vacation. Restless in my spirit, with an irresistible longing to resume singing, I returned to Paris. Two eventful happenings took place during my brief visit there. First, I learned that the other members of The Loving Five were just as eager as I was to pick up our singing career. We found that there was work for us at Lubbock, Texas, where we could earn a livelihood while pursuing our true calling. Consequently, we decided to relocate to Lubbock. It was also during this time that I decided to get married, even though I was barely 19 years old. I had known Willie Belle Pratt since our early school years, and I guess we had always had a puppy-love relationship. Unfortunately, we were to discover later that a stable marriage needs a more solid foundation than adolescent attraction.

The Loving Five didn't exactly make history in Lubbock, but at least we were singing again. We still had some wrinkles to iron out, and we worked on them. I recall the time that Doby Clayburn, who loved to sing louder than anyone else, had a lapse of memory. The lyrics of a particular song mentioned 48 angels, but for some reason, Doby kept singing about 52 strangers. The audience was laughing so hard we could hardly finish the program.

Charles Junior was born during that first year in Lubbock. I was working at the cotton compress and playing football on a semi-pro team called the Lubbock Black Hovers. I must have been a fair athlete, because there was some talk about my playing as a full-time professional. But God called me to sing, and that's what I intended to do! I have found that satan will do anything he can to divert us from the path we should be following. If he can't trip us up with bad things, he'll attract us with pleasant things and try to convince us that they are the right things. They may be good in themselves, but not good for us, not when God has something better in mind. Paul warned Timothy not to get entangled in something that would distract him from his true calling (see 2 Tim. 2:4), and he encouraged the Philippians to choose the best instead of settling for the good (see Phil. 1:9-10). For everyone who has yielded to the allurements of evil and ended up on the junk heap of life, I have seen an equal number sidetracked into accomplishing things that are good and proper in themselves, but sadly and totally contrary to what God wanted them to do. The resulting frustration is a lifelong vexation that robs the deceived of the joy and satisfaction of accomplishment and cheats those other people who would have been blessed by whatever should have been accomplished.

I was supporting my family through menial but honest labor, I was faithful in my church responsibilities, and I was seizing every opportunity to minister in song; but I knew I would never be fulfilled until I was actively engaged in gospel music as a full-time career. As though in confirmation, I experienced a profound spiritual encounter with the Holy Spirit at the Holiness Church in Lubbock when Elder Ford was preaching in a revival meeting. I was raised in church, and I mark my conversion at the age of seven, when I saw the vision that I described earlier. In addition, I was baptized and joined the Methodist Church when I was about 15 years old. However, on this particular night I experienced a personal Pentecost as the Holy Spirit came upon me, and my life was forever changed. From that moment, step by step, the Lord began to take me to a level of spiritual awareness that I had never known before. Even my singing took on a new intensity, as it truly became a form of ministry.

It was the year 1950, and it was apparent that our singing group was about to enter a new phase. We were at a crossroads, and we had to make a decision, based on the feeling that we were to move on to something else. What it was we didn't know, but the answer wasn't long in coming. Shortly after we had moved to Lubbock, a man by the name of Robert Hood had taken a genuine interest in us and befriended us. There were times when we would get discouraged, but he always lifted us up and helped us to believe in ourselves. Before long, however, he relocated to Pasadena, California, and immediately began to encourage us to do the same. The way he described it, we would have limitless opportunities and definitely would have to go full time. I didn't want the responsibility of making the decision, but the group looked to me for guidance. I prayed earnestly and weighed carefully all the factors involved, finally reaching a decision after pondering Granny's teachings about taking a risk when following what we perceive to be the will of God. I had to believe that if I chose the wrong course, God, knowing my obedient heart, would put me back on the right path.

So a small group of young visionaries transplanted themselves from the relative security of the panhandle of Texas to the uncertainty of the golden state of California, settling in Pasadena. I was 20 years old, with the responsibility of caring for a wife and a baby, a family soon to be increased by the births of Patricia, Marilyn, and Susan. We were ready to start anew, full of glorious expectations. At the suggestion of Mr. Hood, we even changed our name from The Loving Five to The Consolators, making a complete break with the past. I wish I could report that we met with instant success—a huge following and more bookings than we could handle. The true story is far different from that idyllic picture. The next few years were a time of constant financial struggle and domestic tension as I sought to make ends meet. For a livelihood I drove a truck delivering furniture, while singing with The Consolators on weekends.

That's the way it went for eight years. Did I misread the Lord's instructions in moving to California? I know it's very easy to confuse your own desires with God's will, but time and again I searched my own heart and asked the Lord to reveal my true motives. I found nothing to shake my conviction that I had acted in sincere obedience to God's will to the extent that I understood it. In retrospect, I see those years as a time of discipline and preparation for the long gruelling years of itinerant ministry to follow. Jesus taught that God would entrust greater things to those who are faithful in small things. I don't know many artists in any field who have obtained instantaneous overnight success without putting forth any effort. Most always there is hard discipline involved, a price to be paid, and nobody who cannot be counted on for the little thing is ready for the big thing.

By 1958 we had reached another time of decision. We needed to be in or out of ministry. In our current situation, we felt we were hindered from reaching our full potential because we were tied to our secular occupations. It seemed that the only difference between Lubbock and Pasadena was a change in address. Since the age of seven I had known God's ultimate path for me. The only uncertainty was the time and the method of getting on that path. Now I felt that I couldn't wait any longer. Singing was my life, and if I couldn't sing then there was no life. I was consumed by the desire to sing the praises of God and to bring a message of hope and deliverance to hurting people. In my present situation I felt that I was walking in disobedience, holding on to an anchor of false material security while in bondage to the circumstances that confined me. I had to sing; I was born to sing; and it was time to do what I knew God had shown me when I was a child. The others were in agreement, and we covenanted together to take the risk of launching out.

It was a costly decision, and had I foreseen what lay ahead for the next few years, I'm sure I would have been much more hesitant. Besides the financial hardships to come, my decision involved the loss of my family. If proper blame is to be fixed in the breakup of my marriage, it should be directed entirely neither to my wife nor me, but to the enemy who is the author of fear and strife. I offer no excuses for myself, nor do I hold Willie Belle accountable. She had struggled with me during the lean years, and the only basis on which I could promise anything better for the future was the solid conviction that I was doing what I was called to do. That unpredictable security was not strong enough for one who needed the assurance of a fixed stability.

I have often been criticized for taking the course of action that I did, even to the point of being charged with selfishly abandoning my family in the name of serving God. The only plea I can offer is that God is my judge, not man, and He knows the genuine intent of my heart. I have tried to do what's right toward Him and toward everyone else, and that includes fulfilling all responsibilities to my family through the years. I have maintained a loving relationship with the children, always striving to meet their every need. It's fruitless to speculate on what might have been if I had chosen differently, but I know that I would not be where I am today. There is absolutely nothing wrong with delivering furniture, but I don't think that was God's purpose for me.

On the other hand, Willie Belle has often been criticized for not following my leadership and supporting me in what I felt to be right. Here again, God is her judge, and no one else has the right to pass sentence on her. Different people have different emotional needs and different personalities, and not everyone can do what I do, or share the lifestyle that I lead. Divorce is a painful ordeal for everyone involved, but it is not unforgivable. Actually, it isn't so much a divorce problem as a marriage problem. If I could help anyone through my own experience, it would be to stress the importance of a man and a woman being absolutely committed both to the Lord and to each other before entering into a marriage covenant. In addition, of course, they should wait for the maturity that will lead them to exercise sound judgment before the Lord. It's far better to wait for that maturity than to pay the consequences of an ill-advised marriage. Two homespun philosophers summed it up very well as they sat on a bench on the courthouse square of a southern town, whittling away a sunny afternoon: "Looks to me like a little common sense would prevent a lot of divorces," opined one of them. To which the other responded, "Looks to me like a little common sense would prevent a lot of marriages!"

So in 1958 The Consolators left California for the open road, all five of us packed into a well-traveled '54 Ford with our entire luggage. We had no permanent home, and we must have looked to a lot of citizens like a modern-day black version of the Dalton gang driving in to terrorize their small towns. As a matter of fact, there were a lot of places where we were not welcome—restaurants that refused us service and hotels that turned us away. Many times we bought gas at a filling station, but couldn't use the rest room or get a drink of water out of the fountain. I can't count the number of times that we washed dishes in a hotel or restaurant and had to visit the bushes out back in order to relieve ourselves. We quickly learned to head for the boardinghouses and cafes in the black section of town. I'll comment more later on prejudice and how we dealt with it.

Those were rough times, but even when we didn't get enough offering to buy the gas to get there, we never thought of giving up. Many times our meals consisted of baloney and crackers at a country store, sometimes varied to include potted meat or Vienna sausages with the crackers. Sometimes we could afford to throw in a little cheese, and I never tired of the old favorites, RC Cola and a Moon Pie. Even now the very thought conjures up the scent of the cotton field. It was not uncommon for one of us to pawn a watch for gas money to get us to the next engagement. There were also times that we would be stuck in a town with no forthcoming engagements, so we would take temporary jobs like dishwashing that paid by the day.

We also experienced many positive features during those days. In 1959 we recorded our first record, *Hold to God's Unchanging Hand*, on the Peacock label in Houston, Texas. It actually did very well, and received nationwide airplay and distribution. The second record, *I'm Going on with Jesus Just the Same*, recorded the next year on the same label, did even better. People began to notice us, and our bookings expanded. Sometimes we would be on the same program as The Swan Silvertones, The Sensational Nightingales, The Harmonizing Four, and The Dixie Hummingbirds, even traveling with them for periods of time. These were groups that had been my childhood favorites, and to appear on the same program with them was a dream come true. It was also during this time that I began writing songs, most of which were drawn from my own experiences, some of which I'll describe later. Not long ago, Mr. Opal Louis Nations, a well-known authority on the history of gospel music, presented me with a tape of all the recordings that The Consolators made. His thoughtful gift is a treasure that brings back prized memories to me.

Just when we were beginning to gain the attention that we had so desperately worked for, The Consolators were forced to disband in the summer of 1960, courtesy of the draft board. We had been like brothers, and we had reached the heights and the depths together. Now we were being sent our separate ways in different branches of the military, except for me. I had been drafted but was declared unfit for military service because of injuries sustained to my knees during my football days with the Lubbock Black Hovers.

So an eventful chapter of my life concluded with the scattering of The Consolators. But as Granny would say, "If one door slam in your face, God goin' open a wider one." And He did.

CHAPTER SIX

SHAKING THE CHURCH

S ometimes it's difficult to understand the ways of God, while at the same time it's very easy to question His way of doing things. I have found, both in personal experience and by observation, that we usually figure things out for ourselves and then think that God ought to agree with us. We decide we know what's best for us, so we work out our own strategy. We convene a committee, we discuss all the options, and we arrive at a consensus concerning the proper course of action. It's a good plan; anybody can see that. Then we pray. And when we do pray, we actually try to convince God that our plan is a good one and that He ought to endorse it. In other words, we view prayer as an instrument to persuade God to come over to our side.

But God doesn't always agree with the systems we devise. I've been around enough to know that God sees the total picture, while our range of vision is limited to our physical sight and finite understanding. So when The Consolators disbanded, I was secure in knowing that God had already marked out the next step and He would make the direction clear to me. Of course, I had known the broad will of

God since I received my calling as a child and had not deviated from it, nor was I about to consider anything else now. The decision I had made when The Consolators hit the road was irrevocable—I was in gospel music, feast or famine. At the same time, however, I didn't want to miss the next phase of God's overall plan. So rather than run ahead of the Lord and try to make something happen that might not be in accord with His design, I decided to take whatever time was necessary to receive an absolute conviction of what I was to do. I didn't know that it would take six months.

But the waiting period was not a waste. In fact, that season was in many ways the most productive time of my life up to that point. Even Jesus felt the necessity to withdraw from the activities of His ministry at certain times for physical and spiritual refreshment. And that's essentially what I did, as I used the last few months of 1960 as a sabbatical in Brooklyn, New York. It was on the way there, just after leaving The Consolators, that I wrote "Travel On," a song that expresses a loyalty to the Lord and faith in His sustaining care in the midst of uncertainty and disappointment. The submissive and determined attitude expressed in the lyrics of the song was tested severely and repeatedly over the following weeks. But God blessed me by reminding me of the vision I had received as a boy and by giving me a greater understanding of the ministry of gospel singing. I saw fields of opportunity far wider than anything I had ever imagined. As my vision enlarged and my conception of ministry matured, an enthusiasm and anticipation that I had never before experienced stirred within me. I was now ready for the next stage of my career.

The Consolators had often appeared on the same program with a well-known group, The Sensational Nightingales. For 15 years they had built a solid reputation and acquired a loyal following. On more than one occasion they had made it clear to me that there would be a place for me in the group if I ever wanted to join them. The timing was right, because when I called them in December of 1960, their lead singer, Julius Cheeks, had just left the group. So in January I became the newest Nightingale, and the lead singer at that. To a lot of people it must have seemed like an untried rookie attempting to replace Hank Aaron. Julius was the most popular of the company, and he was its very heart. Many critics felt that he was irreplaceable and predicted that The Nightingales would collapse with his absence. As a matter of fact, I had some misgivings myself. Julius, or June, as he was affectionately called, had a fiery thundering style of singing. At various points he would take the mike and weave his way through the audience, pointing, stalking, and screaming. No sinner could resist the conviction that fell, and no saint could fail to jump up in rapturous glory. If several groups were appearing on the same program, The Nightingales always appeared last. Nobody dared follow their dramatic performance.

It's no wonder that people questioned my ability to replace Cheeks, since my mellow style was so much softer, and certainly less intense. However, I didn't want to tamper with a formula that had been so successful, so I did my best to fit into the mold that Julius had created. I mimicked his vocal inflections so closely that one listening to our early recordings could hardly tell the difference. But I could tell, and I wasn't happy about trying to be someone else. Besides, I was tearing my throat out by attacking the lyrics in the rough style that had popularized June Cheeks. Something had to change, and gradually it did.

In fact, the change was so gradual that we didn't even realize that it was happening. More and more the group was drifting toward my style of music, which, if analyzed, would reveal a mixture of soul, country, rhythm and blues, and only God knows what else. I began to write more and more of the material we used, and songs like "Wonderful Time up There," "It's Time to Go to the Altar," "Behold God's Face," "I Am on My Way," and "End of My Journey" gave me the opportunity to sing with the spiritual softness and prayerful urgency that had always characterized me. It wasn't long before the group had departed completely from the style it had formally known, and I was in the groove again.

We recorded a string of successful albums featuring more of my songs, such as "His Great Love," "When Jesus Comes," "New Jerusalem," "Going on Just the Same," "He Prayed too Late," "The Love of Jesus," "Son of God," and many others. Although these recordings brought us much notoriety, we turned a gigantic corner about ten years after I joined The Nightingales. I wrote a song entitled "It's Gonna Rain Again," that brought the group to a new level and to a wider and more diverse audience. The song hit the Billboard chart as number one, and it remained on the chart for a hundred weeks. In fact, in the early years of the '70s we had three albums on the Billboard Top Ten chart at the same time—*It's Gonna Rain Again, You and I and Everyone* and *You Know Not the Hour.* Jimmy Dean, Andraè Crouch, and Take Six were among the artists that recorded "It's Gonna Rain Again," helping to bring it into national prominence. I was nominated for a Grammy in 1971 because of this song, which was a candidate for best song of the year. In addition, I received the honor of being nominated the top lead singer of the year. *Jet* magazine selected me as one of the top three gospel vocalists, along with Aretha Franklin and Joe Legun of The Mighty Clouds of Joy.

We were always in a whirlwind of activity, fulfilling a demanding schedule of concerts and recording sessions. Yet some of my most productive years were in those overtaxing times. Instead of being drained by our demanding agenda, I thrived on it and received heightened inspiration that enabled me to write songs that flowed out of my soul. Songs like "At the Meeting," "Saints Hold On," "My Sisters and Brothers" and dozens more originated during that time. One of my most delightful experiences was writing the songs and music for the White Lion Pictograph Production of the movie *Music Box*, a parable featuring a factory worker, five gospel-singing angels (lip-syncing songs sung by The Sensational Nightingales, of course), and a music box. The movie shows in a lighthearted but powerful way how the joy of the Lord can transform a meaningless life of boredom into one that is thrilling and exciting, affecting everyone else. That production received the honor of being named the best Christian movie of the year.

One of the most notable honors I received while I was touring with The Nightingales came in November of 1981. Among its many activities, the nation's museum, the Smithsonian Institute, is charged with the responsibility of preserving and transmitting America's history and culture. That preservation includes the performing arts, to which Black American music contributes a rich tradition, particularly in the areas of jazz, blues, and gospel. In recognition of that contribution, the Institute presented a colloquium in Washington, D.C. on Black American Quartet Traditions, along with concerts by The Sensational Nightingales, The Sterling Jubilees, The Four Eagles, and The Fairfield Four. The program for the event describes The Nightingales as "the best preserved of the 'Golden Age' harmony groups." In addition to the recognition given to the group as a whole, I realized the privilege of having my name recorded in the archives of the Smithsonian Institute as one of the nation's top songwriters in the field of gospel music.

I grew and matured rapidly during the years with The Nightingales, certainly in my personal character, but especially as a professional singer, writer, and performer. More and more I developed a clearer understanding of the nature of gospel singing and the meaning of ministry. I had experienced some mighty lean times, but I always persevered on the path that I had chosen, or rather that God had chosen for me, because to me singing gospel music was more than a way to make a living, more than entertaining; it was a ministry. That ministry began to take me far afield from Paris, Texas, to such places as the Caribbean, North Africa, and many countries in Europe. We sang in churches, arenas, stadiums, concert halls, and just about anywhere else a crowd could be accommodated. Often we appeared on programs with African-American pop and R & B groups.

For some reason, we had become particularly popular in Germany. One of my most unforgettable events took place one lovely evening in an unpronounceable Bavarian town. We arrived at the theater a couple of hours before performance time, only to find the place locked tight. In short time, however, a man arrived and indicated that we should follow him. We didn't have a clue as to where or to what he was leading us, because the only English he knew was "okay." Well, things certainly proved to be okay when we arrived at a restaurant the man owned. In no time at all he had put before us the most sumptuous meal I have ever eaten, even if I didn't know what all I was eating. Rushing back to the theater, we were disappointed to find the place practically empty, with only a little more than 30 minutes until the scheduled performance time. That night I found out that German punctuality is more than fiction, because when we bounded onto the stage a few minutes later, the place was filled to capacity with 2,000 people. Following our performance, we received the loudest and longest standing ovation ever. After five encores we finally left the stage and retired to the dressing room to change clothes. When we came out, the crowd was still applauding. In response, we sang one last song. Putting aside all the hit songs and catchy tunes, we sang the favorite old hymn "Face to Face." The effect on the people was awesome as they stood in reverence and quietly began to file out of the auditorium. To this day, years later, I still hear from people who were present that night.

When I was traveling with The Consolators, we often appeared on the same program with other groups and individuals, a practice that continues to this day. Quite frequently we shared the platform with individual artists such as Mahalia Jackson, Aretha Franklin, Brooke Benton, B.B. King, and with groups such as The Cathedrals. One of my best friends was Sam Cooke, who was the same age as I. In those days, before he went secular, Sam sang with a group called The Soul Stirrers. Not only did we have a professional relationship, but we also spent many hours together jamming and talking, many times in sessions that lasted all night. Our friendship continued even after Sam became famous in the secular pop field, and it ended only with his tragic and untimely death at the age of 33. In contrast to the path that Sam chose, both he and his manager, S.R. Crain, encouraged me to stay in gospel music. S.R. gave me a piece of advice that changed my whole approach to singing. He told me that even though he regarded me as the best gospel singer in the field, he felt that I lacked confidence. He admonished me to believe in what I was singing, and to communicate that assurance to the audience through my singing. I took his words to heart, and ever since, beginning with the very next concert, I have never stepped on the stage without being overwhelmed with a sincere conviction about what I was singing. I can certainly identify with the apostle Paul, who, despite his education and authority, often felt nervousness before he spoke (see 1 Cor. 2:3), but who confessed that he had great confidence because of his great trust in God through Christ (see 2 Cor. 3:4). He elaborated this belief, stating that by himself he could not do anything of lasting value and that his only power and success came from God. In the same way, I know that God has had a call on my life, and whatever success I have known must be attributed to His divine enabling.

I am not one to judge my friend, but despite Sam's phenomenal success in the glamour of the world's spotlight, I often wonder what could have been had he remained true to his calling. I honestly believe that he would be alive today as one of the foremost gospel singers in the world. He asked me to write a pop song for him, which I did, in my only venture outside the area of gospel music. I was in Chicago, where I had an appointment with Sam's brother, L.C., to deliver the song. L.C. never arrived, because of Sam's mysterious death. To this day I have never released that song for publication, nor have I had any desire to stray from the kind of music that is my life.

Over the years I became acquainted with many other celebrities, eventually becoming close friends with several of them. People like Joe Frazier and Red Foxx regularly attended my concerts at Madison Square Garden and Harlem's Apollo Theater. Little Willie John, the well-known blues singer of the '50s and '60s, always came to my concerts whenever he could. He had a hard lifestyle, but confessed to me that he was always touched by gospel music. The boxer Yama Bahama and I became exceptionally good friends, while Lou Rawls became like a brother to me. Others in the entertainment field with whom I have developed a close relationship include Hank Ballard, James Brown, Ray Charles, Clyde McFadden of the Dominos, and Jackie Wilson of the Drifters. With such people I always tried to have a positive influence, and only God knows the impact of those relationships.

The Nightingales were constantly caught up in whirlwind tours, always travelling by car. Anyone knows that six men crammed into the small space of a car for hours at a time have to be on the best of terms, not to mention the fact that they all have to practice good hygiene. I can't think of a better way to test relationships than to travel as we did. It didn't take us long to learn that we couldn't allow irritating things to upset us and that we had to practice a great deal of tolerance. The big things were easy to handle; it was the little insignificant picky things that caused the blowups. It's amazing how smacking gum or cracking a knuckle or clearing the throat or breaking wind can make you want to scream and lead you to the brink of murder. Only by the grace of God can you deal with situations like that, and we experienced that grace countless times.

We each had our assigned seats in the car, and we became as proficient as Larry, Curly, and Moe in synchronizing our shifting positions while we were sleeping. The worse part was when somebody used your shoulder as a pillow and slept with his mouth open. Usually we didn't encounter many problems while travelling, but when you're tired anything can happen. On one trip we were a two-day drive out of California when we stopped to eat about 200 miles past El Paso. When we resumed the trip, Earnest James drove while the rest of us collapsed. I reckon Earnest would have driven us all the way back to Los Angeles if one of us hadn't awakened to find that we were going in the wrong direction, having already passed back through El Paso. More than once a member of the group was left behind at a rest stop while the others, too tired to notice that anybody was missing, went on their way. The highway patrol was usually kind enough not to laugh as they flagged us down and told us to do a head count.

No matter how tired we were before a concert, we always tried to be in top form and give our best. There were many occasions when I didn't know if I had the strength to walk onto the stage, much less extend myself in a taxing intensive ministry for two hours or so, but I really can't remember a time that the Lord didn't provide the energy I needed. We always seemed to be lifted into an element beyond ourselves when we began to play and sing. When the anointing came upon us, as it usually did, we were transported into a heavenly realm, and most of the audience was right there with us. I have never regarded myself as an entertainer; I am a minister. And the people who come to my concerts don't just want to hear something with their ears; they want food for their souls. A preacher communicates with words, and I'd like to think that we singers are just as effective in communicating with our music. In fact, I have seen many cases in which music reached people that words alone could never touch. So although never in my life have I preached a sermon from a pulpit, I look at every song I have written as a sermon, with a message just as effective as one delivered from the pulpit.

Even a mishap can be turned into an opportunity to convey a message. A member of our group for a while was a young tenor named Rudy, who was barely five feet tall. Now what Rudy lacked in physical stature he made up in vitality. I've never seen anybody sing with the emotional zeal that this man displayed. He could cry, laugh, shout, and jump with the best of them, and display the full gamut of emotions in just one song. And when the anointing came, Rudy would customarily run down the aisle shouting.

One night we were performing in a church where the center aisle was carpeted only halfway back, and at that point the wooden floor was freshly waxed, and generously at that. When the anointing struck, Rudy gave a shout, bounded from the stage, and raced down the aisle at top speed. He looked and sounded great until he reached the end of the carpet and hit the wax. In the blink of an eye he was sailing through the air with flailing arms and legs, and he really was doing some shouting then. I wouldn't swear to it, because there was no instant replay, but to this day some people claim that he did a complete flip before he landed flat on his back on that slick, shiny floor.

No bowling ball ever sped down the lane any faster or straighter than Rudy did as he slid toward the back of the auditorium, shouting all the way. The target he was heading for was a high-backed straight chair, one of many brought in to accommodate the overflow crowd. It so happened that a portly lady, wearing a loose-fitting pleated flowery dress, occupied this particular chair. Like an arrow true to the aim of the archer, Rudy reached the mark, right between the sister's spread feet and underneath her pretty flowing dress, coming to a stop only when his shoulders wedged against the rungs of the chair. We could see only his legs, because the rest of his body was imprisoned under the chair and the dress. Naturally, the sister stood up to give Rudy space, but when she did Rudy was nowhere to be seen. All we could see was the violent stirring of her dress as Rudy, lost in its generous folds, was evidently fighting for the surface. Finally, when the lady bent over to check his progress, Rudy managed to crawl out. Now all this time the rest of us were still trying to carry the song that set Rudy off, but because we couldn't make ourselves heard over the ear-splitting laughter, we were forced to stop. Besides, we got to laughing ourselves.

The Lord surely has a sense of humor, and I think He must have enjoyed Rudy's mishap more than any of us. But He also has a way of bringing order out of chaos and driving home a spiritual lesson in every situation, no matter how disastrous it may be. It was that way on this occasion, as the Lord inspired us to make an application of Rudy's demonstration. When the laughter finally subsided to chuckles and titters, we were ready. The lesson was "If You Slip, Don't Slide," that is, if you fall in your spiritual walk, don't stay in that position and keep sliding. Get up and seek restoration. That concert turned out to be one of our most enjoyable and effective.

A personal highlight during my years with The Nightingales began quite unexpectedly. I had been divorced for almost ten years, and

I really had not given much thought to the possibility of remarriage. I had completely dedicated myself to music, and it consumed me. It would take a special woman of great patience and tolerance to share the lifestyle that I had established, and so far I had not met anyone to whom I was attracted. But the Lord has a way of sneaking up on us when we're not looking.

On a beautiful fall day in October of 1967 I was dozing in a barber's chair in Durham, North Carolina, getting a haircut before the next concert. I perked up quickly from my drowsiness when a young lady and two reluctant little boys entered the shop. I later discovered that one of the boys was the lady's brother and the other was her nephew, and that she was actually raising both of them. Something about her bearing struck a chord in me, and the melody has been playing ever since.

Annie Johnson

Now, in natural disposition I'm a shy, retiring person, so there was no way I was going to approach this petite regal lady in a direct manner. I did it the coward's way by enlisting the help of the woman barber who was cutting my hair. She furnished me the information that Annie Lassiter was a nurse in the Renal Dialysis Unit at Duke Medical Center. I had already told the lady barber about the upcoming concert, so I prompted her to ask Annie if she was going to attend. Surely, she would be impressed by my professional status! But no, as a matter of fact she wasn't going to attend because she didn't know anything about it. Furthermore, she had never heard of Charles Johnson or The Sensational Nightingales. Not only did I feel far less important than I did before my haircut, I felt about 20 degrees cooler from the icy chill coming from the direction of Annie Lassiter.

Even after such a frosty brush-off I was still intrigued by this striking woman to the extent that I couldn't dismiss her from my mind. I'm over six feet tall, but a delicate woman of 5'1" had completely overpowered me. However, it was obvious that she didn't have the slightest interest in me. We had another concert scheduled at a church in Durham the following February, but never did I entertain the thought that she would be there. But God's grace is not only abundantly sufficient; sometimes it's a total surprise. It turned out that this was the church that Annie attended, and she was at the concert! Never before did I sing with as much gusto as I did that night after I spotted her in the audience. I guess I have to plead guilty to glorifying self instead of the Lord. Anyway, God surely forgave me for trying to be so impressive, because after the program Annie and I had the opportunity to talk. I surprised myself by asking for her telephone number, but I was even more surprised when she gave it to me.

As time passed, Annie and I enjoyed many cordial visits, mostly by telephone, but occasionally over dinner. As our relationship developed and I came to know her better, I began to appreciate her many fine qualities. Besides the fact that she was attractive and virtuous, she was blessed both with unusual intelligence and a sanctified common sense. She was also generous and compassionate, and she was every inch a lady. She would be an ideal wife, and I knew it. Finally, she did become my wife in August of 1972, and she has more than fulfilled the role of a helpmeet. She has stood with me through times of want and times of plenty as companion, secretary, accountant, agent, editor, nurse, cook, and countless other roles.

No children were born to us, but shortly after our wedding we adopted Jody, Annie's five-year-old nephew, and Nicole, her three-year-old niece. She already had had custody of them and had been a mother to them since they were toddlers; after our marriage we made it official. Although we never legally adopted him, Anthony, Annie's five-year-old brother, also became a vital part of our family. And a vast emptiness in my life was abundantly filled.

At this point I want to pay tribute to Annie's mother, a precious and devout saint of God named Beatrice Lassiter. She was well into her eighties when, after a lingering illness, she died in August of 2001. The day before she died, she matter-of-factly told Annie that she was going home. The next day she slipped into a coma and was completely unresponsive. I had never heard this dear lady sing in all the time that I had known her, and later Annie told me that she could not remember her mother ever having sung. Suddenly, however, as we were standing by her bedside, this comatose woman began to sing in a pure, sweet, youthful voice the words of "Precious Lord, Take My Hand." Her voice gradually faded as she neared the end of the song, and shortly thereafter, without regaining consciousness, she peacefully went home with the Lord. "Precious in the sight of the Lord is the death of His saints" (Ps. 116:15).

CHAPTER SEVEN

TURNING SORROW INTO JOY

During the years that I had been travelling, first with The Consolators and then with The Nightingales, I lacked the opportunity to see much of Granny, but I never forgot or strayed from her teachings. Of course, I received regular reports about her, and there were infrequent opportunities to visit with her, such as the first time she came to hear me sing professionally. Granny never lost her mental capacities or her physical vigor, in spite of her advancing years. Her undimmed eyes still sparkled, and her thick hair was only speckled with gray. Her posture was unstooped, and her unhurried steps were straight. Even in her final years her skin was remarkably unwrinkled.

This extraordinary woman had endured much, especially during the years of bondage in slavery, but she never lost her zest for living, nor did she ever express regret for anything in her life. I recall how as a boy I would get furiously angry with those who had wronged her when she recounted stories of her youth. Yet, she told of her experiences without any hint of malice, and she always had an object lesson in mind as she spoke. She enjoyed the blessing of life itself more than any other person I have ever known, and she certainly squeezed every drop of joy from each day's offerings. "Life like a mirror," she told me. "It don't give back no more than what we put in it." Well, she put her full capacity for living into each day, and she received a generous daily dividend on her investment.

However, there were times that I detected a faraway look in her eyes and a pining in her voice when she spoke of things from the vastness of her past. Sometimes when she didn't know anyone was around, I watched her as she sat on the porch, looking as though she was seeing right beyond physical time and space. Every so often I would hear her talking to someone when I didn't see anybody within listening range. I finally asked her what she was thinking and looking at, and who she was talking to. In response to the first question, she told me, "I'm lookin' at things that can't be seen, and I'm thinkin' things that ain't, but ought to be." Now that didn't make a bit of sense to me, so I asked her how in the world she could see and think things that ain't.

"You can't, if it's 'in the world,'" she said. "But I'm talkin' about things that ain't in this world. Just 'cause you can't see it with yo eyes and hear it with yo ears don't mean it ain't there. There are different ways to see and hear."

She was saying that there is a spiritual reality that is not open to the physical senses or to scientific investigation, a reality that is even more real than the physical, and that can be detected only by spiritual insight. Such a concept was out of the range of my boyish understanding, of course, so as usual she had a story to illustrate what she was talking about. She reminded me of something that happened in the life of the prophet Elisha, described in Second Kings 6:8-17. The king of Syria was certain that there was a spy in his organization, because the Israelites knew his every move, and consequently they were always prepared for his strategies, no matter what they were. However, his advisors assured him that no one had betrayed him; instead, there was a prophet in Israel who had established a hotline to Heaven and received news of the king's plans direct from God.

Well, the solution to the problem was obvious—God's mouth-piece had to be eliminated. So the king sent an entire army to surround the city of Dothan, where Elisha was staying. Now Granny had a manner of describing things in such a way that I could visualize the whole dramatic scene. She told how Elisha's servant had been fixing breakfast and went out to get some water to make coffee. Granny's dramatic account enabled me to see what the servant saw and to feel his fright as he gaped at the thousands of chariots of war, headed by fierce snorting horses stamping their impatience to race into battle, and filled with the meanest-looking soldiers imaginable, armed with the finest weapons of war. The terrifying sight sent the servant running to his master to stammer out the news, with the obvious conclusion that any thought of escape was hopeless.

Elisha didn't seem to be disturbed at all. Stifling a yawn, he calmly advised the trembling servant, "Don't worry about it; those that are for us are more than those that are against us." The servant "knowed that 'Lisha done lost his mind, 'cause ain't nobody out there 'ceptin' the whole Syrian army, and they ain't got no reason but one for bein' there." So the prophet prayed for God to open the servant's eyes and instructed him to return and take another look. Reluctantly, the servant did so. At first everything appeared to be just the same as before—chariots, horses, soldiers, and weapons. But as his spiritual eyes were opened, the servant was able to look beyond the limitations of physical sight into ultimate reality. And what he saw defied anything he could possibly imagine. The hillsides were covered with the mighty hosts of Heaven, ready to do battle on behalf of God's prophet!

Granny didn't know the meaning of the word *theology*, but no biblical scholar could have a better understanding of God's ways than she had. And that faraway look I saw in her eyes so many times had its gaze fixed on something much closer than any physical object. She was peering into the heavenly realm and keeping company with angels. Paul spoke about "the eyes of the heart being enlightened" (see Eph. 1:18). Granny possessed that kind of vision, and that's how she could see "things that ain't."

Actually, I was inaccurate when I described Granny talking to someone who wasn't there. Just because I couldn't see anybody didn't mean Granny was talking to herself. One day I sneaked up close enough to the porch to hear what she was saying. She was sitting in her old rocker, snapping beans and talking to God! Now I really couldn't call it praying, because it just didn't sound like the begging and pleading and praising and moaning and groaning that I had always associated with praying. To me, it wasn't praying if you hadn't worked yourself up to such an emotional state that God was bound to hear you for the volume, even if He didn't agree with what you were saying.

But here was Granny, talking quietly with Him, just like He was a familiar neighbor sitting next to her over a bushel of beans. I reckon she didn't leave anything out of the conversation, covering everything from baby Jewel's colic to the current international crisis. I believe she knew she wasn't telling the Lord information He didn't already know; she was simply discussing things with Him. I was gripped most of all by her expressions of thanksgiving, spoken with such simple sincerity that the Lord couldn't fail to be touched with its genuineness. There was no flattery, no repetitious sugary phrases attempting to impress God. Surely her plainspoken, "Lord, You been mighty good to me, and I'm much obliged," meant just as much to Him as the loftiest anthem offered by a cathedral choir. As a matter of fact, when Granny would hum a hymn in the solitude of the front porch of a ramshackle country dwelling, I could just picture the scene in Heaven as God turned to the majestic angelic choir and said, "Shhh, be quiet, I want to listen to this!"

In her conversations with the Lord, I would often hear her speak of her long lost sister Sarah. She was convinced that her twin still lived, and apparently she had been faithful in praying for her every day for scores of years. And even now, as unlikely as it could happen, she maintained not only the desire, but also the expectation, of a reunion with Sarah. Granny never considered the impossibility of something she believed, particularly if there was a biblical precedent. And here there was. "Lord, I know You done let Joseph see his daddy again, when he don't know if he dead or alive, so I know you goin' let me see my sister 'fore we both meet You face to face." Talk about "hope against hope"!

I have to confess that as a boy I never felt the intensity of my grandmother's desire. My world didn't extend more than 15 miles beyond Paris, Texas, and my family circle already had a huge circumference, what with cousins I haven't counted to this day. And as the years skipped by, I thought even less of Granny's fondest hope. As far as I know, nobody made any attempt to locate Sarah, even given the remote possibility that she was still alive. Where and how would you begin? Besides, who cared?

Well, evidently God cared, especially in matters pertaining to a chosen daughter with whom He was intimately acquainted. And He knew that "hope deferred makes the heart sick, but when the desire comes, it is a tree of life" (Prov. 13:12). Granny's hope had been deferred for a hundred years, ever since two bewildered and frightened young sisters had forlornly gazed each other out of sight through tear-filled eyes from the backs of wagons going in different directions on rutted, dusty Louisiana roads heading toward Alabama. And long after they lost sight of each other, each still cried out for the other. I don't have a clue why God took so long to answer Granny's prayer, because I know He heard her. I began to gain a little understanding years later when I read about somebody else's hope that had been deferred.

Luke 1:5-25 tells about a priest named Zacharias and his wife Elizabeth, who had prayed for a child for years, finally giving up when both of them were well advanced in years. But one day while Zacharias was ministering in the temple, the angel Gabriel appeared to him with the startling news that his wife would bear a son. In making his announcement, Gabriel told Zacharias that God had heard their prayer when they first uttered it, and now He was going to give what they had requested. I heard a preacher explain that the verb *heard* literally means *heard-to-do*, indicating that when God heard their prayer He said "yes" to it right then and there. Now, years later, He was going to give what He had already granted. And Zacharias and Elizabeth became the parents of John the Baptist. In a similar experience, an angel told Daniel that God had granted his prayer when he first offered it, but the actual giving of it came three weeks later (see Dan. 10:12-13).

Surely God has a reason in delaying to deliver what He has already bestowed. Maybe He answers later in order to answer better, or perhaps in some cases He waits until the situation becomes humanly impossible. Then He intervenes in such a way that there is no doubt who accomplished the feat, and therefore He receives all the credit and the glory.

Whatever the explanation of the delay might be, Granny finally received that for which she had been doggedly praying for so long, and only God could have directed the way it happened. For more than 60 years, Granny had lived in Lamar County, Texas, ever since the Johnsons had banded together with the few other families in migrating from Alabama. As far as I know, she had never been out of the county until 1957, when she went to Oklahoma City to live with my Aunt Etta and later with my sister Mary, who had also moved there. Thus, Granny's great-grandchildren were blessed with the same privilege that had been mine, growing up with the teachings and personal example of this extraordinary woman. They have vivid memories of what they learned, and I received from them confirmation of many of the recollections that I have related in this book.

Aunt Etta was the mother of my cousin Ezell Kendrick, who had given me the opportunity to make my singing debut with The Harmony Kings, and who had made it possible for me to work on the ranches in Texas. After he moved to Oklahoma, Ezell began singing with a group called The Soulseekers. While giving a concert in

Louisiana in the early '60s, he unexpectedly received an indication that Granny's sister might still be alive, as well as a clue to her whereabouts. A lady spoke to him after the program, commenting on the fact that she felt she knew him, especially since he looked so much like her son. The conversation revealed that the woman's mother had an experience strangely similar to what had happened to Granny. She too had been sold into slavery, along with a sister whom she never saw again. Unfortunately, because of a family separation when the lady was only a child, the only other information she had was the possibility that her mother lived in Oklahoma. His interest aroused, Ezell visited others in her family, including the woman's son, who indeed bore a striking resemblance to him. However, he was unable to learn more about the mysterious ex-slave, and returned home disappointed but with much to ponder.

Happily, the cold trail in Louisiana grew hot back in Oklahoma. A certain man had been regularly attending The Soulseekers' concerts in the Oklahoma City area for about five years. Gradually, he and Ezell struck up an acquaintance, and Ezell invited him to his home for dinner. The man drove into the front yard, got out of his car, and walked toward Granny, who was sitting in her accustomed spot on the front porch. The nearer he came to her, the more astounded he became. "You look exactly like my mother, Sarah," he exclaimed. The story he proceeded to tell was so parallel to Granny's experience that there seemed to be only one logical explanation. Could it be, after a hundred years and more, that Granny was to receive a positive answer to her prayers for a reunion with her sister? The only way to be certain was to get the two venerable ladies together. The only problem was to keep Granny from bursting with impatience until that time.

As soon as arrangements could be made, Ezell drove to El Reno, Oklahoma, where Sarah lived, and brought her back to Oklahoma City. What followed was a scriptwriter's dream, and the drama of it would tax the abilities of the finest actresses to portray it. I guess nobody realized the significance of the event at the time, so the reunion was completely without fanfare, which is exactly the way Granny would have it. This was the early '60s, well before the days of video cameras, but nobody even thought to capture the moment with a still camera.

Granny rose from her porch chair in anticipation as the car turned into the driveway and slowly made its way into the yard. By the time the car came to a stop she had descended the three steps of the porch and stood waiting for the answer to a hundred-year-old prayer. Two ex-slaves faced each other in a brief instant of awkward uncertainty, as though the moment could not possibly be a reality. Not a word was uttered as two pairs of arms reached toward each other to span the lost years of separation. There, under the shade of a giant elm tree, the sisters embraced for the first time since they were cruelly torn from each other more than a century before, and all the past pain and grief were swept away by the joy that engulfed them. Ezell said it was the only time in his life he had ever seen Granny cry.

The sisters had two days together, and the time belonged strictly to them, even though it could hardly begin to compensate for generations of separation. How can you summarize the stories of two centenarians in only a few hours? It was enough for the sisters merely to be together, and each evidently knew it was to be the first and last time. Granny's parting words to Sarah were, "Next time we see each other, we don't have to say good-bye." Although they corresponded with each other, through the writing and reading of children and grandchildren, they never met again.

Their lives had had a striking parallel. Both had left Alabama for Texas after the war that freed the slaves and both had spent their days on farms and raised large families. Both had been active midwives, and both were renowned for their homespun wisdom. And both died within two years of their reunion.

I was on tour, and news didn't reach me of Granny's departure until after her funeral. I had never known her to be sick, and she never even showed the ordinary decrepitude of old age. She just didn't believe in getting sick. But in the last months of her life, a persistent pain and a nagging weariness indicated that an intruder was draining the strength of her body. The diagnosis was breast cancer. Were it not so serious, it would have been laughable. By best estimates Granny was in the neighborhood of 115 years of age in 1966, the year of her death. All those years she had been immune to the ravages of disease and the deteriorating process of advanced age. To think that it finally took breast cancer to stop her! Actually, it wasn't the cancer that killed her; it was complications from surgery. She faced the ordeal with her usual disposition: "Well, that be just another river to cross." Apparently, she came through the operation in fine fashion and was recovering beyond expectations, when she contracted an infection. Pneumonia set in, and the aged heart that had served her so strongly and so well for so many years finally gave up. Crossing this river brought her straight to the portals of Heaven.

She was buried in a cream-colored dress trimmed in lace, looking every bit like the queen she was in life. The legacy she left will endure until time is no more. I haven't bothered to try to number her descendants, because it would be an exhaustive task. There are hundreds of us. I can only pray that in the writing of this book I have been able at least in some small measure to memorialize such an uncommon woman. I anticipate a joyful reunion after I cross that final river, and I expect our voices of praise to join in perfect harmony. Meanwhile, I'll keep on singing "Another River to Cross," a song I wrote when I was contemplating Granny's positive viewpoint, which describes the life of Christians as a journey through our temporary dwelling place on earth to our heavenly home. There are often obstacles to overcome, pictured as rivers to cross, but Jesus help us along the way. Finally, after the Lord takes us safely across the last river at the end of the pilgrimage, He leads us into our eternal home to dwell with Him forever.

I was still with The Nightingales when my mother died in September of 1978, at the age of 83. She had shown symptoms of heart problems, and tests confirmed that she must have surgery. She was admitted to the hospital, but she died on the operating table. Her very best friend, with whom she visited daily, died the same day. Mama had prayed fervently that all her children would be saved before she died, and so they were. Not long ago, a movie was released entitled *Big Momma's House*. The producers had to be thinking of my mother, because all her grandchildren affectionately called her "Big Momma," and it was always a treat for them to visit Big Momma's house.

My mother's death left a greater emptiness in my life than even Granny's. She had been my best friend all my life, and we had always enjoyed a close relationship. As I have previously indicated, she was firm in discipline, but she was always fair and reasonable instead of

Mama's House

rigid and unbending. She would always give an explanation of what she was doing, and she took time to teach me moral lessons. After I reached adulthood and looked back, I could see clearly how Mama never exercised discipline in a rage, but always in a longsuffering love, with a view toward correction. When she said something, she meant it, and all of us knew that her word was law. And we accepted it without argument, whether we liked it or not, because we respected her and her judgment. She never had to browbeat us or manipulate us, much less bribe or beg us. No child ever had a better role model than she was to me.

Mama did her best to fill the void in my life created by the absence of a father, and because of her efforts I did not feel deprived in any way. I maintained such a deep respect for her and wanted to please her in every way I could. On Saturdays, when everyone else went to town to have fun, I stayed behind. That was my day to hunt for rabbits, squirrels, wild turkeys, or whatever other game I could find to supplement our food supply. I didn't mind those hours of solitude, because during those times of communion with the Lord, He built my character and planted seeds in my heart that would later blossom into songs.

Because of my respectful obedience to my mother, I earned her reciprocal trust. Just as I believed her when she told me something, she believed me when I told her something. Not only did she believe me; she believed *in* me. She never doubted that I had a divine call upon my life, and she always gave me sound counsel and assuring encouragement. She never thought it to be foolish and idle day-dreaming when I talked of being a gospel singer, and she never sought to dissuade me by telling me I better get practical and learn a trade or take up farming in order to earn a decent living. Nor would she tolerate any mocking harassment of me on the part of others. She believed in me to the point that she revealed to me that she never had to worry about me. "You my heartstring," she used to tell me.

Of all that Mama taught me, two lessons stand out above all else. First, she impressed upon me the importance and worth of integrity in everything that I do, say, or write. Forever ingrained within me is her penetrating admonition: "When you sing, make sure you mean what you sing; otherwise you will be singing a lie." If all churchgoers followed that counsel, how many would have to remain silent while the rest of the congregation sang "I Surrender All" or "Wherever He Leads I Will Follow," or dozens of other hymns? Not once have I written the lyrics of a song apart from the remembrance of Mama's stirring words. Heaven won't be what it's supposed to be unless my mother can say to me, "You done what I told you." You see, even years after her death, I still want to please her.

The second instruction Mama deeply instilled in me was the conviction that I could overcome the impossible. She never spoke negatively to discourage me in my youthful quest to become a gospel singer. On the contrary, she led me to believe that "with God all things are possible" (Mt. 19:26), and that through faith "nothing will be impossible for you" (Mt. 17:20). At the same time, she showed me that achieving a goal meant more than closing my eyes and dreaming or wishing. There was stern discipline and hard work involved, and she did all she could to help me along the way. I think back to the time that I scrimped and saved to buy my little record player and some records. Every penny was crucial to our family, and we all contributed. But Mama, seeing how desperately I wanted this small luxury, forestalled any guilt of selfishness I might have felt by telling me, "That your money. You done earned it, and you got a right to use it any way it help you."

I declare to you that no poverty can crush dignity. The only thing that can repress a person is an acceptance of circumstances, with the threadbare conclusion, "That's the way things are, and there's nothing we can do about it." If everybody subscribed to that theory, people like me would still be in slavery. I encourage you to accept my mother's challenge to attempt the impossible, if you feel a divine leading, and exert all your energies to accomplish it. Nothing is impossible to you if God is with you. If God be with our weakness, it becomes strength; if He be with our foolishness, it becomes wisdom; if He be with our fear, it becomes courage. Put God into a boy's hand, and although he may have a giant to battle with, he'll be able to use the weapons of sling and stone to lodge the stone in the giant's head. Put God into man's arm, and while his only weapon may be the jawbone of a donkey, he'll slay the enemy in heaps. Put God into a man's eyes, and he'll flash defiance on rulers of earth and hell. Anoint a man's lips with coals from Heaven, and he'll speak truthfully and boldly, even in the face of death. Every second you delay will add fuel to the critics' taunts. Get busy and get at it. The only thing that can guarantee your failure is your inaction. Don't accept the verdict of skeptics who say you can't do it. I'm living testimony that you can overcome the odds and reach your goal, and I thank God that I had a mother who lifted me up instead of put me down.

CHAPTER EIGHT

SINGING GOD'S TUNE

Despite the success I was enjoying with The Nightingales, I was far from content, feeling a lack of fulfillment. I became more and more aware of the fact that there was another level for me to reach. I certainly wasn't unhappy with the others in the group, because we maintained the congeniality of brothers. I just felt stifled, because I had no room to grow and expand or develop in the way that I desired. I suppose that such a feeling is much better than existing in a comfort zone, thinking there isn't anything else to accomplish. I have observed over the years that when people think they have arrived, they usually have; that is, they don't progress any further. Fulfilling a divine call is something like riding a bicycle—you keep moving or you fall off. A person who has something stirring in his soul, which God has put there, remains unsettled until there is a release of whatever is there. If God puts a song in my heart, I can't rest until I give expression to it in lyrics and music.

I believe it's possible for a person to be financially successful and have power and prestige apart from God, but he won't have the fulfillment that he might have had. A locomotive is built with a certain nature, and as long as it operates according to that nature, it can accomplish powerful feats. It was created to run on railroad tracks, but suppose the locomotive begins to feel hemmed in and suppressed by being confined to the tracks? What if it looks out across the wide fields and decides on its own to leave the tracks? The moment it leaves its intended path, disaster strikes. Its power becomes useless, because it isn't where its maker designed it to be. God has ordained tracks for us to follow, and we can reach our full potential only as we are in accord with His will.

I know that God was trying to encourage me to take the path He had laid out for me. Even so, I struggled for seven years before I finally made that move. It's easy to tell someone to step out in faith, but it's quite another thing to leave the certainty of a solid security that you have known for years and venture into the unknown and untested. I had a lot of questions to consider, but I suppose my reluctance can be summed up by a fear of that unknown factor. When I look back, I marvel that I could ever doubt the faithfulness of a God who had called me in the first place and who had proved Himself again and again. In reality, there was only one thing that I should have considered, and that was what God wanted me to do. I have since learned that when God wants you to do something or be something, He places at your disposal all the resources of Heaven that are necessary to enable you to do or be what He desires. In other words, God's commands are always accompanied by His enabling. I also learned that faith is the key that opens the door to all those enabling resources.

But how can you hear from God in order to know His will? I want to share with you some principles I discovered from my own experience that may help if you are wrestling with a decision. First, we must have a readiness to obey God even before we know what He wants us to do. Most people make decisions as if they are a jury. They listen to all the facts and then consider them. If the facts seem reasonable, they act accordingly. But God doesn't deal with us on that basis, because His will isn't on trial. Our attitude should be, "Lord, I don't know what You are going to say to me, but I commit myself to obey what You say even before You speak it." We sign a blank contract and let God fill in the details.

Why is it so difficult for us to relate to God in this way? Is it because we are afraid He'll take advantage of us and pull some low-down trick on us? Suppose your son said to you, "Mom and Dad, from now on I'm going to do everything you tell me to do, and I won't argue about it or ask you why." What would your reaction be, that is, after you recovered from the shock? Would you think, "We've finally got this boy right where we want him. What's the meanest, most diabolical thing we can tell him to do?" Of course you wouldn't. And "if you then, being evil, know how to give good gifts to your children, how much more will your Father who is in heaven give good things to those who ask Him" (Mt. 7:11).

Choosing readily to obey expresses our faith in a loving heavenly Father. But God will not reveal His will to us if we demand that He first allow us to glance at the script and then let us decide whether or not we will obey. We must commit ourselves to obey even before we know what He wants us to do or where He wants us to go. The stance of "tell me what it is and I'll decide" never prevails with God.

Knowing that God's will, whatever it is, is always best, we submit to it in advance, before we are aware of what it is.

In addition to a readiness to obey, we must have a willingness to listen. These principles are listed in the correct order, because if we have already decided not to obey, we are not going to listen to anything God says. It's impossible for a disobedient spirit to hear clearly from God, but one who is obedient is eager to hear. An unruly student doesn't have a teachable spirit. The best piano teacher in the world can't help a student who debates and defies everything the teacher says.

We must listen with an attitude of obedience. We are not to listen in order to argue with God or evaluate what He says, and certainly not to offer suggestions or alternatives. We listen because we are determined to obey. I believe that people hear exactly what they are prepared to hear. Sometimes they think that God isn't speaking, when in reality they are not hearing. The problem is not in the transmitter, but in the receiver. If God wants us to do something, it's His responsibility to communicate it to us and impart to us the means to do it. Our responsibility is to hear and act. We can be certain that God will do His part. Our part is to adopt the attitude, "Speak, for Your servant hears" (1 Sam. 3:10).

Sometimes God may have to position us where we have no choice but to trust Him. When Moses was leading the Hebrews out of Egypt, many of the people preferred whatever security their bondage in Egypt provided over the uncertainty of a dangerous trek across an unknown wilderness. So God had to prod them to move. With mountains on both sides and every Egyptian soldier in Pharaoh's army swooping down from behind, only forward was left. And forward was the Red Sea, which is exactly where God told them to go. Their only choice was to trust God or be slaughtered by the Egyptians, or at best be delivered into bondage worse than what they had previously known. So they went forward. But do you think they would have taken one step toward the sea if the Egyptian army had not been thundering down upon them, forcing them to do so? Not on your life.

Well, God had to prod me into action. The relationship between The Nightingales and our record company had gone sour. We were not getting the airtime that we should have, and the company was lax in promoting us. I definitely felt that something shady was going on, and it became an intolerable situation for me. Instead of the peace and joy that the ministry should have brought me, there was only drudgery. I wanted out, and I told the others that I was leaving in three months. The moment that I made that announcement, the load lifted from me and a rush of peace engulfed me. I knew that I was doing the right thing, even though the others tried to talk me out of it. We had gained a tremendous notoriety, and they didn't understand why I wanted to leave such success, especially since I had no definite plans. All I knew was that I was acting in obedience to God, and I couldn't look back. There were no hard feelings, and I continued to maintain a cordial relationship with the group. I was pleased some time later when I read how Jo Jo Wallace, a long-time Nightingale, responded when an interviewer asked him about my departure. He replied, "Charles Johnson is a unique writer and arranger who believes in the Word of the Bible. He left The Sensational Nightingales to spread the ministry in different areas."

I parted company with The Nightingales on December 12, 1983, after having been with them for 23 years. I had no bus, no bookings, no equipment, and no certain knowledge of the future. All

I had that belonged to the past were memories and a guitar, and concerning the future all I had was my trust in the Lord. However, I soon discovered the truth of the old adage that "where God guides, He provides." Jesus doesn't want us to be paralyzed with fear and anxiety, so He tells us in Matthew 6:25 not to worry about what we shall eat or drink or wear, because our heavenly Father will see to it that we have all those things. The climax of His admonition is in verse 33: "But seek first the kingdom of God and His righteousness, and all these things shall be added to you." In other words, our concern is not to be with the physical and the material, but with the spiritual. A person cannot seek first the things of God if his mind is preoccupied with the things of this world. As Jesus tells us in Matthew 13:22, the cares of the world and the deceitfulness of riches (the mistaken notion that wealth can erase the cares of the world) prevent the Word of God from bearing fruit in our lives.

Why does God promise to supply all our needs (see Phil. 4:19)? The reason is not that we may merely have all we need. After all, even unbelievers can have their needs supplied. We all know plenty of unbelievers who have bigger storehouses of supplies than we have. The main reason God promises to provide for our material needs is so we can be free to seek Him and His Kingdom. Remember that while He is also concerned about our physical life, His primary concern is with the spiritual. If I don't have to worry about my physical needs, I can give all my attention to seeking and serving Him. That's what God wants—freedom for us to concentrate on His will and righteousness. And He gives us that freedom when we entrust our physical and material needs to Him.

It didn't take long for God to demonstrate His faithfulness. Only two or three days after leaving The Nightingales, I received a visit from Mr. and Mrs. Roy Willis, a couple who had attended many of our performances. The Lord surely sent them, because they really didn't know me very well. Even so, Mr. Willis asked me if there was anything I needed. He emphasized his sincerity and encouraged me to tell him my needs right then and there. How could I refuse an offer like that? I provided Mr. Willis with an extensive shopping list, but he didn't bat an eye. He furnished me with a van, a sound system, a bass guitar, and suits for my group to wear at concerts, even though I had no group and no bookings. This couple asked nothing in return for their generosity, not even repayment. As far as they were concerned, they were presenting me with an outright gift. With the Lord's help, I was to repay them within two years.

Even though I had the equipment I needed, I didn't have a group to use it. I guess that really didn't matter, because neither did I have a place to use it, nor did I have a promoter or booking agent. I have to admit that I met a lot of temptation to discouragement, and some people very close to me urged me to give up the idea of a new group and go back to the tried and proven. Many fellow artists tried to convince me that I could never be successful with a new group and with the style I wanted to sing. We shouldn't be surprised when satan uses others to discourage us. After all, he used Peter to try to discourage Jesus. I praise God that my decision had already been made. I had put my hand to the plow and wasn't about to look back. With rather strong affirmation, I announced that I would live by myself in the woods before I went back.

I decided I had better form a group first and then be concerned about bookings. A young man by the name of Darrell Luster kept coming to my mind, so I contacted him. From the age of 12, Darrell had often opened shows for The Nightingales, and his talent, dedication, and enthusiasm had always impressed me. Not only did he respond with interest, but he was instantly enthusiastic about the idea of being part of a new singing group. He called his brother Rick, and the three of us spent hours together practicing every day. Darrell played lead guitar, Rick handled bass, and I played rhythm in addition to singing lead vocal. To our delight and amazement, we found from the very first that we blended in perfect harmony. For the first time, I felt I had the opportunity to arrange things personally in my career. I didn't know or understand anything about southern gospel, inspirational, contemporary, or any other labels applied to "white gospel music." I just wanted to write, sing, play, and minister my own style of music.

After three weeks we felt ready to hit the road. We still lacked a fourth member, but we were confident that we could find pick-up musicians to fill out on drums and keyboards. Only one thing held us back. Despite our shiny equipment, our new name, our dedicated preparation, and our intense eagerness, we didn't have a place to sing. However, God's timing is perfect. As I've said before, He is faithful to carry out His responsibility if we are obedient to His will, and once again He proved Himself. It was early in January of 1984, and we had just wrapped up our final practice. "Well, we're ready," one of the brothers commented. "But is anybody ready for us?" I replied that God didn't bring us together just to sing to each other. If He anoints somebody to sing He's going to provide an audience. I didn't realize how prophetic my words would prove to be.

The next day I received a call from a man by the name of Raymond Whitten. When he asked for me, I assumed that he must have been trying to contact The Nightingales and said so. "No," he replied, "I want to talk only to Charles Johnson." It turned out that

Mr. Whitten had seen *The Music Box*, the movie for which I had written the music and in which The Nightingales had sung the voices of the angels. He was so impressed that he called the production company to get my telephone number. He had no way of knowing that I had left The Nightingales and formed a new group. It proved to be an eventful call, setting in motion a series of engagements that has continued to this day.

Mr. Whitten invited us to sing at his church in Malvern, Arkansas. Other invitations followed in rapid order. Our benefactor took care of us for the next 19 days and arranged 19 bookings for us during that time, all of which paid enough to launch us on our new career. We found gracious favor everywhere, even in unexpected ways. On one occasion, we were stranded in an ice and snow storm while we were on the way to a concert in Memphis. We took refuge in a motel, where the owner charged us nothing for staying there.

After 19 days of going out from Malvern, we travelled to West Virginia. A church there had invited us on the recommendation of Mr. Whitten's church. We gained immediate popularity there also, and invitations came rapidly. Later, our recording of "Going on with Jesus" was played every hour on radio stations in that state, where it became the most popular song. Many bookings resulted from the airtime we received.

Before 1984 had passed, The Revivers had recorded their first album, entitled *No Man Can Stand Alone*, produced by Malaco. Later we entered into contract with Better-Way Records, with whom we completed our first video production in 1988. Recorded live before a packed house of wildly enthusiastic fans at Memorial Hall in Dayton, Ohio, we entitled the video *One Night Revival*, and it truly was a night of soul-strengthening revival. Other videos soon followed, including *He Hideth My Soul* and *Let's Have Church*. We enjoyed a string of hit audio releases with Better-Way, including "Sealed till the Day of Redemption," "Mansion over the Hilltop," "Until Then," "The Time Is Drawing Nigh," and "I Can't Even Walk Without You Holding My Hand." Each of these songs hit the charts, and "I Can't Even Walk" climbed to the top five on the Singing News charts.

The success that we experienced was not automatic, and it was not without dedicated hard work. I didn't even know what the term *Southern Gospel* meant. I simply wrote what I felt and we sang it the way we felt it. A turning point in our ministry came with the popularity of "Sealed till the Day of Redemption" in 1988. A Southern Gospel radio station gave it a great deal of airtime, and other stations quickly picked it up. The widespread recognition of that song created an entirely new listening audience of white people, who started demanding more.

The demand was met with "I Can't Even Walk," which captured the attention of Nashville record companies. I signed with Canaan Records, a subsidiary of Word, in 1991, and a new series of best-selling albums resulted. All the singles from the Canaan releases *Let's Have Church*, *We Cannot Stand Alone*, and *I Believe* were hits on the Southern Gospel charts. People who had never heard of The Revivers were buying our tapes. We were rapidly gaining thousands of new followers, and attendance at our concerts was swelling. The same pattern of success continued after we entered into an agreement with Centergy Records, which released *Hymns* and *Good Time in the House*. We had gained such notoriety that Roseanne Barr even used one of our songs on an episode of her television series.

A lady by the name of Betty Foley Cummings was a big fan of mine. A daughter of Red Foley, the legendary Grand Ole Opry singer, and the sister of Shirley Boone, Pat's wife, Betty and her husband Bob learned to know me because I appeared many times on the same program with their son Clyde. She surely paid me the highest compliment possible when she told me that I sang "Peace in the Valley" just like her father. Betty and Bob revealed to me that they had made a pact, stipulating that when one died, the other would have me sing that song at the funeral. When Betty died, I did indeed sing at her funeral, and it was one of the most humbling and touching experiences I have ever had. After the funeral, Shirley came to me and told me that she wanted me to sing at her funeral as well. I responded that she might be the one singing at mine!

I reckon that over the years I have experienced just about anything that can take place during a concert. I have described some of the humorous incidents, and there have been many more, just as there have been countless dramatic happenings. I have witnessed undeniable miracles on many occasions, such as the one in Conyers, Georgia, when a large tumor suddenly disappeared from a lady while she was praising the Lord during a concert. Only God knows how many people have been healed spiritually. A typical testimony is that of a woman in Jackson, Tennessee, who attends every one of our concerts in that area. The first time she attended, she fell under such heavy conviction that she repeatedly tried to leave the auditorium. According to her, "a strong power," which we know was the Holy Spirit, held her back. She did not leave until she had surrendered her life to Jesus.

We have had plenty of detractors in attendance as well, but they are no match for the sovereign God. During a performance at a church in Rome, Georgia, a burly man who could pose for a recruiting poster for the Hell's Angels was sitting on the third row, next to the aisle. He was big enough and strong enough to chew me up and spit me out, and it looked to me like that's exactly what he had in mind. I was convinced of it when all of a sudden during the fourth song of the concert he jumped to his feet and started running toward the front. I frantically looked around for a way to escape, but before I could move the man dropped to his knees at the altar and began crying out to God in repentance. Afterwards he told me that the only reason he came was to ridicule and disrupt the service. However, beginning with the very first song the Holy Spirit brought such a heavy conviction upon him that he could stand it no longer.

I am living testimony to the reality of Isaiah 54:17: "No weapon formed against you shall prosper." In the middle of a performance at the Ryman Auditorium in Nashville, Tennessee, a man interrupted by jumping to his feet and screaming, "Charles, I've tried to hurt you and destroy your career for the last 12 years, but I want to repent to you and to God." Right then and there he experienced a dramatic conversion. Now I have no idea what the man had against me, but the driving force behind him was satan himself. However, a child of God doesn't have to walk in fear, but always in the assurance of the protective presence of God.

I have been blessed with the protection and favor of God all through my career. In the spring of 1991 we were in the midst of a concert in Kentucky, when we heard the sound of a mighty rushing wind. I wish I could tell you that we were experiencing Pentecost all over again, but this wind was quite literal, in the form of a tornado. The roof of the building where we were singing was completely lifted and sent sailing like a kite, but not a person was injured. Scores of vehicles in the parking lot were smashed, but there wasn't a scratch on our car.

One of our most prized instruments was an L-5 Gibson guitar, the same as Elvis used to play. Along with other equipment, it was stored in a luggage carrier atop our car while we were driving on the beltway around Washington, D.C. Those of you who have never had the thrill of driving on that highway don't know what you are missing, and those of you who have had the privelege will find it difficult to believe what happened. The luggage carrier with its precious cargo was swept away by a strong gust of wind and went bounding down the highway and then across six lanes of traffic. Surely an angel was guiding its pathway, because it evaded collision with at least a hundred cars before it came to a rest. We finally worked our way over and stopped by the side of the road, dreading the sight of the shambles inside the carrier. To our amazement and gratitude, not one item had suffered damage!

I have also learned that God bountifully provides for our needs. On one occasion early in 1959 The Consolators were in Pittsburgh, Pennsylvania, without a cent among us. We had not eaten for two days, because what little money we had was just enough to buy the gas to get us there. I took a walk while we were waiting for time to prepare for the performance, and I sniffed the most heavenly fragrance I had ever smelled. It was the sweetest incense ever offered in sacrifice. Its aroma far surpassed the essence of earth's most aromatic flowers, all gathered together in one lavish bouquet. I was enchanted, and there was no way I could resist the alluring temptation to trace to its source the wafting balm that beckoned me with its tantalizing appeal. I found it just around the corner, but it might as well have been a thousand miles away. There in the plate glass window of a neighborhood deli-restaurant, for the entire world to see, was a slowly spinning rotisserie, laden with the most succulent golden chickens I have ever seen. I stood transfixed watching the drip of the life-giving juices, savoring their taste as my imagination licked them from my fingers. At that moment I came closer to committing a felony than at any other time in my life, and had a brick been handy, I might have resorted to some window breaking. As it was, I inhaled deeply and forced myself to back away, praying for an offering large enough to feed us. We really didn't have to worry, because one of God's servants invited us to her home for a snack after our performance. She didn't know how hungry we were, but she had a pretty good idea after we cleaned out her refrigerator and pantry.

I've experienced God's bountiful provisions so many times that when a need arises, I simply turn it over to Him. I'm not being presumptuous; I'm just doing what God has told me to do. If I'm about His business, then it's His responsibility to supply my needs, just as He said He would. And I've discovered again and again that God keeps His word. Most often He uses individuals through whom He can channel His blessings. Like the time The Revivers were at a church in West Virginia, with little money and a bus badly in need of repair. Immediately after the news of our predicament became known, a mechanic offered free labor to fix the bus. However, we didn't even have money to buy the parts. But when God starts a job, He finishes it. Another man came forward and paid for everything we needed. God takes care of His people!

It hasn't been easy staying on the road, but the certainty that I'm doing what God has called me to do and the ministry that I have fulfilled make it all worthwhile. Through all the rough times, my mainstay has been Isaiah 43:2: "When you pass through the waters, I will be with you; and through the rivers, they shall not overflow you. When you walk through the fire, you shall not be burned, nor shall the flame scorch you." My experiences have taught me that Jesus is not a bridge over troubled waters; He is a pathway through them.

CHAPTER NINE

HARMONIZING WITH HEAVEN

S ometimes people ask me where I get ideas for the songs that I write. Actually, I don't get them; they get me. In other words, my songs are not the product of my head, the result of my own ingenuity or natural ability; they come straight from my heart, born of actual experience and emotion and planted there by a reality other than myself. I know that it's possible to produce literary works or art or music with a natural skill, but if it isn't touched with the passion of one's soul, then it's nothing more than cold professionalism. For example, how many sermons are grammatically perfect and delivered with grand eloquence of speech and persuasive logic, but are nothing more than impressive oratorical displays, because there is no divine fire inflaming either the message or the messenger? How many times have you heard a singer present a song with magnificent voice control, perfect pitch, and wonderful clarity, but the presentation doesn't stir you, because you know that you have been listening to a polished performance completely untouched by the passion of soul? And I believe that a true artist is one who is able to transfer to the canvas what he sees and feels deep within.

I cannot write a song unless it is born of a thought, an experience, or a feeling quickened by the Holy Spirit. In fact, I don't even want to sing a song that I don't personally feel. I've got to be honest, and there is no way I can communicate otherwise. What Heaven puts into me I want to put out in the form of music, and for that to happen I have to be in constant harmony with Heaven. Sometimes it may take only minutes for a song to come forth, but more often than not, the idea has to lodge in my heart for a period of nourishment and reflection before I'm able to give expression to it.

In one way I wish I could tell you that I was born with a flair for writing, and that I was a child prodigy, able to dazzle people with the amazing ability to churn out dozens of songs at will. However, it's far better that it wasn't that way, because, as I have stated, my songs are born of experience and are a direct communication from my heart to yours. I always feel an urge to tell people things, and I've learned very early that the best way for me to communicate a message is through songs. In fact, I believe that the most widely used vehicle of communication worldwide is music. Just look around at the people listening to music and check the statistics on the sales of musical products. In my case, people who wouldn't walk across the street to hear me talk will drive miles to hear me sing. And can you imagine how many millions of people are receiving messages, whether good or bad, through songs at this very moment?

I wrote my first song in 1959, when The Consolators were going through a tough time. We were stranded for a month in Hot Springs, Arkansas, lacking funds to continue traveling. During that time I worked in the kitchen of a Holiday Inn. To this day I haven't found anybody who can explain to me why I could wash the dishes that white people ate from and why I could prepare their meals, but I couldn't use the employees' rest room. How could that possibly contaminate the customers? At any rate, I had to go out the back door and head for the bushes whenever nature called. There were other indignities I endured, some of which I'll describe later, and they kept piling on top of all the other discouraging trials I was enduring at the time. What do you do in a situation like that, when you feel that everybody and everything is against you, and apparently God is too busy looking after other business to give attention to your problems? I could wallow in self-pity and curse society in general and God in particular for the ills inflicted upon me. I could certainly justify my actions if I struck back in some way, whether in crime or seething hatred. And the easiest thing would have been to abandon the idea of a career in gospel music and get a steady job. I admit that I was tempted to do all those things, but I couldn't do any of them. I had made my decision, and I wasn't going to be dissuaded. So squarely facing the opposition and the circumstances, I steadfastly affirmed, "I'm going on with Jesus just the same," and God knew I meant what I said, come what may. With that declaration the words of a strong resolution flooded my heart, which I translated into a song entitled "Going on with Jesus:"

Chorus

I'm goin' on with my Jesus just the same;
I'm goin' on with my Jesus just the same.
You may false accuse me, scandalize my name,
but I'm goin' on with my Jesus just the same.

Verse 1

The narrow way is a straight way;
it don't have no crooks and bends.
I got to go on with my Jesus,
I know he's my best friend.
When my enemy's all around me, tears fill my eyes,
I'll bow down on my bended knees
and I'll rise up with a smile, and say,
"I'm goin' on with my Jesus just the same."

Verse 2

Somebody may laugh
and talk about me when I shout,
but this is one thing for sure,
I know what I'm shoutin' about.
When old Satan try to stop me,
put stumbling blocks in my way,
I stand up, fold my arms, and these are the words I say
—I tell him, "I'm goin' on with my Jesus just the same."

By reading the words of this song and knowing their background, perhaps you can begin to understand what I mean when I talk about expressing my heart. The attitude communicated by those words has been my mainstay through all kinds of difficulties, and this song has been my confession of faith in rough times.

A particularly difficult time came when The Consolators disbanded because of the military draft, a situation I mentioned earlier. I was in a state of confusion, because I thought we were living in God's will. But just when we were enjoying some measure of success, everything seemed to collapse, and I questioned if it all had been in vain. My commitment to stay in gospel music remained firm, but I had to get away to seek the Lord about my next step. On the bus to New York I was contemplating the circumstances, when a profound peace filled me with a warm glow deep within my soul. There came to me the assuring voice of God: "Son, I put you on the road where I want you to go. You just keep travelling on and I'll prepare the road." Keep travelling on! Don't worry about where the road goes, because if God laid it out, you'll always be heading in the right direction. Within minutes, while barrelling down the interstate in a sleek Greyhound, I had written on scratch paper words that welled up out of my heart.

Those simple words, which were published as the song "Travel On," give voice to a resolute determination to remain faithful to God's calling, even in the midst of bewildering and disappointing struggles. Through the years many people have testified that this song gave them a renewed perseverance in keeping to the path in which they felt God had directed them, even in the midst of discouraging circumstances.

Lyrics don't always come instantaneously. Sometimes the seed of a song has to stay in the heart for a long while, germinating until the time is right for it to blossom. For more than six months I had been meditating on the fact that we cannot stand alone and we need to lean on the Lord for support. I knew the Holy Spirit lodged the thought in my heart, but try as I might to expand it into a song, the words never came forth. Then at three o'clock in the morning on our first of three days in Richmond, Virginia, the Lord awakened me with the words of the first verse of "We Cannot Stand Alone."

Verse 1

I was undone, I could not stand,
until Jesus reached down and took my hand.
He picked me up, he rescued me,
and everything I try to do,
I put my Jesus out in front of me,
because we cannot stand alone, cannot stand alone ...
no matter how hard we try,
we can't make it on our own.

I was flushed with excitement that I had the beginnings of a powerful song, so all that day I tried to write the second verse. But all I felt was a stony wall of silence. Exactly at 3:00 a.m. the next night, I awakened again and immediately penned the second verse.

Verse 2

A man is born in sin, you see,
and he is shaped in iniquity.
He is corrupt deep down within—
our Bible plainly tells us,
brother, we must be born again,
because we cannot stand alone, cannot stand alone,
no matter how hard we try,
we can't make it on our own.

This time I knew I could continue on my own, so all day I worked on the next verse. But, as the song says, we can't do it on our own. For the third consecutive night, I awakened at 3:00 a.m. and effortlessly wrote the third verse.

Verse 3

It's so good to have,
when you're sleepin' at night,
someone to stand by your bedside
and keep everything just right...
who can wake you
in the mornin' right on time,
who can start you out on another day's journey
clothed and in your right mind.

I guess God must have chosen such an hour because that was the only time He could get my undivided attention. Or maybe He was showing me that I could produce nothing except what He put into me, and that truly I could not stand alone. As Jesus stated in John 15:5, "Without Me you can do nothing." I know that the Lord "gives songs in the night" (Job 35:10), and just when I was beginning to think that was the only time I could write, God switched to daylight time.

From time to time, when I feel depressed,
and it seems for me there is no rest,
oh, I take my all and all and to Jesus I go ...
he's a wonderful friend, and he steps right in,
just when I need him the most,
because we cannot stand alone, cannot stand alone,
no matter how hard we try,
we can't make it on our own.

I don't know how it is with others, but most of my ideas for songs come when I read the Scriptures and meditate upon what I have read.

For example, the story that Jesus told of the rich man and Lazarus (see Lk. 16:19-31) gripped me with the tragedy of waiting too late to pray. I wanted to echo the warning of Jesus in a way to bring conviction to heedless people, and the result was "He Prayed Too Late." The song recounts the failure of a haughty man to give any consideration to God and to serving Him during his lifetime, but who was full of remorse in his eternal state after he died. It's urgent to live righteously before God in this world, because death gives no second chance.

A woman once requested me to sing at her husband's funeral. I agreed and asked her what song she wanted me to sing. She must have known something the rest of us didn't, because her request was "He Prayed Too Late."

Even that request didn't surprise me as much as the next one, when I asked the widow what she wanted the group to sing. "Well," she said, "my husband's favorite song was 'Jingle Bells.' " Now to me that just didn't seem to be an appropriate melody for a funeral, but I reckoned that we had to respect the wishes of the bereaved. But how do you fit "Jingle Bells" into such a solemn occasion? The preacher and I decided that the spot where there would be the least disruption was at the very last, at the gravesite just before the interment. You don't know how I hated to announce to a bunch of mourners under a sweltering July sun that we were going to sing "Jingle Bells." But we did it, even though the song was never sung with less enthusiasm than on that occasion. Afterwards the widow came up to me and asked, "Did I say 'Jingle Bells?' I meant 'When They Ring Those Golden Bells.' " Life does go on, even after humiliating experiences.

The song that brought me to the forefront in gospel music was "It's Gonna Rain Again," which was on the Billboard chart for a hundred weeks, and was number one for much of that time. As I stated previously, it was nominated for a Grammy. When I wrote the song I had just read again the story of Noah and the hard-hearted heedlessness of the people in the face of impending judgment. In my meditation I realized that conditions today are just the same, and people go on their way without giving any thought to the finality of judgment. So in simple words I modernized the story.

Way back in the Bible days,
Noah told the people, "It's gonna rain."
But when he told them, they paid him no mind,
and when it happened, they were left behind.

They tell me when the water began to pour,
they knocked on the window, they knocked on the door.
They didn't know exactly what to do...
You don't want this to happen to you.

Noah said, "I'm sorry, my friend,
God's got the key; you can't get in."
If somethin' don't happen to the hearts of men,
the same thing is going to happen again.

Noah told the people in plenty of time,
but they were too sinful, and they were too blind,
and when it came that awful day,
they tried to pray, but their prayer was too late.

I tell you, it's gonna rain, it's gonna rain...
You better get ready and bear this in mind.

God showed Noah the rainbow sign;
it won't be water, but fire the next time.

I have never sought to categorize my songs, and very rarely have I planned beforehand to write a song on a certain theme. I just respond to what I'm feeling, and in doing so, I touch upon many themes pertaining to salvation and living the Christian life. Many of the songs are warnings of judgment and a call to repentance, such as "He Prayed Too Late" and "It's Gonna Rain Again." Once when I read the solemn words of rejection spoken by Jesus, "I never knew you; depart from Me" (Mt. 7:23; see also Mt. 25:41; Lk. 13:27), I reflected on the thoughtless living of millions of people who somehow think they can avoid God's judgment. The result was a song entitled "Giving You a Warning Sinners," which describes unrepentant sinners facing God's wrath. Even though they seek refuge wherever they might, there is no escape. The song calls to mind the vivid scene portrayed in Revelation 6:15-17: "And the kings of the earth, the great men, the rich men, the commanders, the mighty men, every slave and every free man, hid themselves in the caves and in the rocks of the mountains, and said to the mountains and rocks, 'Fall on us and hide us from the face of Him who sits on the throne and from the wrath of the Lamb! For the great day of His wrath has come, and who is able to stand?' "

Because of personal experience and the teachings of the Bible, I firmly believe in the power of intercessory prayer, particularly in praying for the unsaved. God desires that all people repent and receive salvation (see 1 Tim. 2:4; 2 Pet. 3:9), so when we pray for someone's salvation, we are praying within the revealed will of God.

God spared Lot from the destruction of Sodom and Gomorrah because He remembered Abraham's intercession (see Gen. 19:29). The intercession of Moses saved Israel from the judgment of God (see Ex. 32:11-14). God instructed Eliphaz and his two friends to go to Job and let him pray for them so that they might be spared (see Job 42:8). In light of these truths, I wrote "It's Time to Go to the Altar." Here are the chorus and first verse:

Chorus
It's time to go to the altar.
It's time to go to the altar and pray.
It's time to go to the altar and pray
For the ones who have fallen by the way.

Verse 1
Preachers and teachers that are carrying the word today—
they are twisting it and turning it in so many different ways.
They talk about the way to heaven, but there is only one.
If you want to see the Father, you've got to go through by the Son.

Despite society's acceptance of abortion on demand, I believe it's an abomination, subject to severe judgment. Out of my grief and anger over this hellish practice came the song "You and I and Everyone."

Chorus
You, I and everyone—
we've got to stand before our God;
we've got to stand at the judgment
to be judged for the deeds we've done.

Verse 1

On that resurrection morning,
when Gabriel blows his horn,
we got to stand at the judgment
to be judged for the deeds we've done.
Now, when you face the judgment bar,
there'll be no one there you can ask for help;
when the roll is called up yonder,
you've got to stand there for yourself.

Verse 2

Our Bible teaches us to multiply,
and to multiply means giving life;
but so many people in the world today
are tryin' to change that way.
They make believe that it's not wrong
to take a life before it's born,
but every seed you sow by the way
is comin' up in the judgment day.

I particularly enjoy writing songs that encourage Christians who are suffering difficult times. We can think of life as a voyage. We are sailing on the sea of time between two eternities. And the circumstances of life are like the weather. Sometimes there is smooth sailing, and at other times there are storms. We will always encounter a storm when we are sailing contrary to God's will, but many times we also find ourselves in a storm that is beyond our control. For example, sickness or financial difficulties may come; there may be business setbacks or disappointments in a relationship; or countless other trials may assail us. In situations like that, people need more than someone to tell them, "Well, good luck. Hope things work out." I want to remind people that we possess something substantial to survive the storms of life. The same Lord who faced a raging storm and commanded, "Peace, be still" (Mk. 4:39), can still calm the tempests that threaten to overwhelm us. Through my songs I want troubled people to know that Jesus is there to guard them through the storms of their life, to give them joy to gladden their hearts even in the midst of the storm's mighty blasts, and to grant wisdom and power to guide them every step of the way, though the path be darkened by the storm clouds of their life. I know what I'm talking about, because I have experienced what I sing, and I can testify that the songs are true. That's the message of "My Hand in His Hand," the first verse of which declares:

Verse 1

I was standing alone at the crossroads;
I was caught in the middle of the storm;
I couldn't see either direction;
I didn't know which way to turn,
but along came a friend
who saved me in troubled times.
While I was holding to His hand,
He was holding mine.

The same affirmation of faith sounds forth in the second verse:

Verse 2

There's no other friend
like the One that's holding my hand.
He promised He would go with me,
even to the end.

143

And all along the journey,
when my hills are hard to climb,
I can hold to His hand
while He's holding mine.

In "Winds of This World" I describe how Jesus is our shelter in spiritual attacks as well as in physical trials. I know very well what the Bible means when it says that "the devil walks about like a roaring lion, seeking whom he may devour" (1 Pet. 5:8). After one particularly strong attack by the enemy, during which I followed the instructions to "resist him, steadfast in the faith" (1 Pet. 5:9), these words flowed out as an encouragement to others going through similar battles:

Jesus is a fence around His children;
His grace is sufficient to stand the storm;
His word is a promise we can stand on,
when the winds of this world is a'blowin' strong.

Old Satan is movin' to and fro
throughout the land, seeking whom he may devour;
but he was defeated at Golgotha
that day when Jesus made him out a liar.

Old Satan is always sneaking around
the gate tryin' to lead a sheep astray,
but He that is in us is so much greater than he;
so, then rebuke him and chase him away.

If you are caught out in the winds of this world
with no joy in your life at all,

just give your heart to Jesus; He'll always understand,
and He will never, never let you fall.

Jesus is with me when the storm clouds gather;
He's standing by my side when I hear the thunder roll.
He holds my hand when I begin to tremble,
when the winds of this world is a blowin' strong.

When we think of all Jesus has done for us, we are assured of the power of His love. I was overcome by deep gratitude and humiliation as I reflected on that love, and I wanted to pay tribute to the Lord for pouring out His love on someone as undeserving as I. The result was "The Love of Jesus," whose chorus declares:

Chorus
His love is higher than the mountain;
His love is deeper than the sea.
I pray to the Lord each day
for a closer walk with Thee.
It's more precious than silver;
it's more precious than gold.
That love of Jesus is well with my soul;
that love of Jesus is well with my soul.

Jesus has done everything possible for our salvation. But how is the world to know about His sacrificial love? As far as I know, God has only one plan to spread the good news. Jesus commissioned His followers to go throughout the earth to tell people what He has done (see Mt. 28:18-20; Mk. 16:15; Lk. 24:46-49; Jn. 20:21; Acts 1:8), and Paul said that we are ambassadors of God, charged with the responsibility of telling people about the reconciling work of Jesus (see 2 Cor. 5:18-20). We are the ones God is depending on to tell the story, so how are people to know if we fail to obey? I asked and answered that question in a song entitled "Who Should Remember?"

Verse 3
Now, there are so many who have strayed from the fold;
some of them are young, and some of them are old.
Who should seek for them through the storm and the cold?
We that know Him are the ones.

Chorus
Who are the ones? (We are the ones.)
Who are the ones? (We are the ones.)
We who know Him
are the ones.

I have always been struck by the emphasis the New Testament places on the fact that there is only one Body of Christ, one family of God, regardless of social, cultural, and racial distinctions, not to mention denominational rivalries. In light of these plain teachings, God cannot be pleased that in the Church we still maintain these natural barriers to fellowship and continue to separate ourselves from each other. I expressed His displeasure in a song entitled "God Is Not Pleased." The song describes God's grief over the disharmonious, competitive spirit among His people that puts self over the needs of others and seeks to advance self at the expense of others. Then it expresses God's desire for His people to exhibit the self-giving spirit of Christ.

Having experienced discrimination, about which I will write later, I emphasized the oneness of the church more strongly in "My Sisters and Brothers." No believer in Christ can belong to Him without belonging to other believers as well. If they are children of God, then they are brothers and sisters, and the New Testament makes it clear that love for brothers and sisters in the Lord is not an option, something we can choose to do or not do as the mood strikes us. The last command Jesus gave before His betrayal was that His followers should love one another, not in some vague and undefined way, but just as He loves us, that is, with a self-sacrificing love that involves service (see Jn. 13:34). In the context of that command, He acted out a parable of love by garbing Himself as a servant and washing the feet of the disciples. I tried to picture that same spirit in my song.

I particularly enjoy writing about Heaven, when we will see the Lord and experience a family reunion throughout eternity. Here are two verses and the chorus of "Holy City, New Jerusalem," expressing that expectation:

Chorus

Holy City, New Jerusalem,
coming down from God out of Heaven;
Holy City, longing for you;
we shall see the King in His glory.

Verse 1

When we enter the gates of that City,
all the saints of God will shout, "Victory."
It will be the beginning of a reunion
that will last throughout eternity.

Verse 2

We can walk down those golden streets together
with our hearts rejoicing, set free.
It will be so good to know that we will be there
with our family throughout eternity.

I've reflected a great deal on how it's going to be in Heaven, and the older I get, the more precious Heaven becomes. I know that Granny, Mama, and my sisters are waiting for me. I've written about that great meeting in Heaven in several songs. Here are the chorus and one verse from "Jasper Walls":

Chorus

This road we now travel is narrow;
this road we now travel is long.
It leads on to the pearly gates,
on to where the streets are paved with gold.
There we're going to see that crystal river
that flows from the throne that God and the Lamb sit on.

Verse 1

This mean and evil world we live in,
how the heart of man has grown so cold.
Sisters and brothers hating one another,
many sheep have strayed from the fold.
Christians and friends, let us take each others' hands
and turn our faces to the eastern sky,
and let it be known that we're soon going home,
for the day of redemption draws nigh.

That expectation is expressed even more strongly in the following verse and chorus from "I'm Going to the Meeting":

Verse 1
When I leave this world behind me;
when I've gone to come no more;
when I sing my last song,
I'm gonna move to my brand new home.

Chorus
Some day soon, I'm leavin';
I'm going to the meeting around the throne.
I'm gonna shout, "Trouble's over,"
as soon as I move to my brand new home.

No American old enough to understand news reports will ever forget the heinous terrorist attacks of September 11, 2001, that forever changed our lifestyle. Providentially, in the spring of that year we recorded a patriotic video entitled *A Nation Under God*. Javetta Saunders, who produced the video, and Miller Goodman, who directed it, did a masterful job of capturing the spirit of America. The video features stirring footage of American landmarks and songs by The Revivers that cannot fail to cause a lump to well up in the throat and quicken the heartbeat of every person who loves this country. The title song calls us back to our spiritual roots:

Verse 1
A nation under God was the foundation
until the enemy came and convinced we should not pray,
and the place where we build the future
now the strong winds are blowing it away.

149

Chorus

A nation should be built on the Rock of Ages.
The Rock of Ages is known to stand the test of time.
It will never decay; it will stand through eternity,
and there's no wind will ever blow it away.

Verse 2

A nation should not be built on sinking sand
or without the true foundation below,
for without the foundation strong it will not stand the storm.
The strong winds will blow it away.

Verse 3

There are some who still say, "Why should we pray?
We're living in a modern and enlightened day."
But when the call came to pray no more,
"In God We Trust" walked out the door,
and the strong winds are blowing it away.

Surely it was no coincidence that this video was released the same week as the terrorist acts. The song quoted above soon climbed near the top of the charts.

It would take far too much space to refer to all the songs I have written. The ones I have mentioned are representative of them all, and the others emphasize one or more of the themes reflected in them. Someone once asked me which of my songs I would like to be the last one that I sing. I responded without hesitation, and later I'll reveal which song it is and why I want it to be my departing act.

CHAPTER TEN

LIVING LYRICS

Someone once said that he had rather see a sermon any day than to hear one. He was talking, of course, about the testimony of people's lives. It is a fact that people influence one another, for good or bad. I honestly believe that if people related to each other according to the teachings of the New Testament, society would be much more harmonious, life would be much sweeter, and we would have on earth a foretaste of Heaven. I have always been impressed by the fact that Jesus, knowing that He had only a few hours to live (see Jn. 13:1), chose to give as His last commandment to the apostles before His arrest, "Love one another, as I have loved you" (Jn. 13:34). The fact that He spoke these words in the form of a command tells me that we have no choice in the matter. If we are in obedience to our Master, then we are not going to turn on other people and "judge" them (Rom. 14:13); "lie" to them (Col. 3:9); "bite and devour" them (Gal. 5:15); "provoke and envy" them (see Gal. 5:26);

"speak evil against" them (see Jas. 4:11); or "grumble against" them (Jas. 5:9).

The kind of attitude expressed in these prohibitions typify the world's way of relating to each other, which is built on the principle of "me first." A lot of people mistakenly think that they can lift themselves higher by pushing others down, and so they take every opportunity to promote themselves while trying to make the other person look bad. In contrast to this practice, the Bible tells us to "build up one another" (see Rom. 14:19) and to "do good" to each other (Gal. 6:10; see 1 Thess. 5:15). Our relationship with others is not to be characterized by a spirit of rivalry, bitterness, or envy. On the contrary, we are to "be kindly affectionate to one another with brotherly love, in honor giving preference to one another" (Rom. 12:10). From that statement it seems clear to me that we are to be self-forgetful, while placing others before ourselves, and that's hard to do when we are living in a world that teaches us to put ourselves first and to look after our own rights and privileges, places and prestige. However, this command must be important, because Paul repeats it in Philippians 2:3-4: "Let nothing be done through selfish ambition or conceit, but in lowliness of mind let each esteem others better than himself. Let each of you look out not only for his own interests, but also for the interests of others." He backs up this charge with the example of Jesus, telling us in verse 5 to have the same attitude that the Lord displayed when He willingly gave up the glories of Heaven to come to earth and die for us.

Jesus commanded us to love one another as He has loved us (see Jn. 13:34). To enforce this command and to demonstrate the kind of love we are to have, He acted out a parable of love by performing a servant's duty of washing the feet of the disciples. Now that tells me that love doesn't simply involve speech; it includes concrete acts of kindness. Love is not a sugary sentimentality or a passive negativism that does no evil to the other person; it always issues in active sacrificial service. Jesus applied the lesson of the footwashing in John 13:12-17, and in particular He said, "I have given you an example, that you should do as I have done to you" (v. 15). That's why He called His command to love "a new commandment" (v. 34), because He is the standard of love. It wasn't beneath the dignity of Jesus to clothe Himself as a slave, get down on His knees, and humble Himself in the service of others. Is it beneath ours? Christ expressed the ultimate of love in John 15:13: "Greater love has no man than this, than to lay down one's life for his friends." True love always gives to serve; it sacrifices itself in order to serve others. Following the example of Jesus does not mean that we are to wait around for the opportunity to perform heroic deeds of self-sacrifice, because life is full of opportunities to do all kinds of acts of goodness. Love is seen in the doing of the little things as well as in more spectacular deeds—the giving of a cup of cold water in the name of Jesus (see Mt. 10:42), the small touches that can mean so much.

John asked, "But whoever has this world's goods, and sees his brother in need, and shuts up his heart from him, how does the love of God abide in him?" (1 Jn. 3:17) He then adds in the next verse: "My little children, let us not love in word or in tongue, but in deed and in truth" (1 Jn. 3:18). This passage tells me that if we relate to others with the love of God in us, we will see their needs. I think that means more than a casual glance, like the "certain priest" who took a quick look at the man who had been beaten and robbed on the Jericho

Road and then hurried by on the opposite side (see Lk. 10:31). Christian love causes us to see the needs to which selfishness is blind.

This passage teaches us that divine love enables us to feel the needs of others, instead of closing our hearts against them. In contrast to the priest and the Levite, who "passed by on the other side" when they saw the helpless victim, we are to have the attitude of the Samaritan, who "when he saw him, he had compassion" (Lk. 10:31-33). If we have the love of God in us, the sight of need will always arouse our compassion. Many times we read that Jesus "was moved with compassion"—by the leaderless or hungry crowds (see Mt. 9:36; 15:32), by the sick and the blind (see Mt. 14:14; 20:34), by a single leprosy sufferer (see Mk. 1:41), by a widow who had lost her only child (see Lk. 7:13). "Therefore, as the elect of God, holy and beloved," let us "put on tender mercies, kindness, humility, meekness, longsuffering" (Col. 3:12).

First John 3:18 tells us that it isn't enough to see and feel the needs of others; we must act to relieve those needs. Christian love is positive, always seeking the good of others, even at personal cost.

I believe that God does not intend for us to live our lives in isolation, building barriers that seal us off from one another. He designed us to live interactive lives, so that we are dependent on one another, as individual members of the body relate to each other. He meant for us to live in fellowship, to touch each other's lives, to help each other along life's journey, to influence each other for good.

Thus, I have just laid a foundation for paying tribute to some people to whom I am indebted, for helping me during my life's pilgrimage. Every person is capable of giving and receiving influence, either for good or bad, and either consciously or unconsciously. And to some degree an individual is molded and shaped by the contributions of others. That's certainly true in my life, and I want to acknowledge some of those people who have poured themselves into me. They will be only representative, because I cannot possibly identify the countless men and women who have made me what I am. I have already mentioned a few of them, such as Mrs. Donnell, Robert Percy, Robert Hood, Mr. and Mrs. Roy Willis, and Raymond Whitten.

Although I have briefly expressed my profound esteem for my Aunt Ella's husband, Uncle Benjamin Harrison Kendrick, I must underscore what I wrote earlier. The best and most accurate description I could give of this remarkable man is a repetition of what was said of Barnabas in Acts 11:24: "He was a good man, full of the Holy Spirit and of faith." Can anything greater than that be said about a person's character? If everybody had a character like that of Uncle Harrison, the world sure would be a good place to live. I never had a relationship with my natural father, but this man could not have been more of a father to me. He had six children of his own, yet he treated me as one of his own. If ever there was a worthy example of honesty and disciplined industry among men, this man was it. He lived to be 99, and almost until his last year he was still driving his pickup truck, filled with the equipment by which he plied his trade of yard work. When it comes to dependability and stability, Uncle Harrison was the Rock of Gibraltar. I really do think that he considered it a sin if he didn't do more than he was expected to do when performing a job. He taught not just by words, but by example, and he taught so well that his lessons still impact my actions, those of his six children, and those of many others who learned from him.

He meted out discipline that was firm but fair, exercised more toward correction than punishment. He would never tolerate excuses for failure to do your best. He thought people were foolish and deceptive if they promised what they knew they couldn't deliver, but on the other hand he commended people for making an honest effort to accomplish whatever was within the range of their capabilities. He was a man of his word, and he accepted at face value the word of others. He felt that a community could not exist on suspicion and distrust, and even the fact that others often took advantage of his trusting attitude did not deter him. He looked for the best in people, and he didn't think anyone was beyond redemption. Just because an individual had the privilege of humanity and possessed whatever dignity humanity conferred, surely there was some worth in that person. At least that's what Uncle Harrison thought. Someone once challenged this view by describing a particularly obnoxious person who was a blight on society and completely devoid of anything worthwhile. Uncle Harrison responded that such a person could always serve as a bad example!

I have also mentioned my childhood teacher, Mrs. Maggie Reese, but she deserves a much greater expression of appreciation than I have already given. I guess the days of a one-room schoolhouse served by a pitifully underpaid but fiercely loyal Mrs. Reese are gone forever. But spacious modern buildings, gleaming laboratories, and the finest technical equipment don't necessarily guarantee the best education. Teachers are the ones who teach, and beautiful buildings and state-of-the-art equipment are no substitute for common-sense wisdom administered by a dedicated Mrs. Reese, with a stick of chalk in her hand, a blackboard behind her, and a paddle on her desk.

She didn't just teach facts; she taught us what to do with the facts we learned. She gave her students a compass, infusing what they learned with purpose, so they would know where they were going in life. She constantly emphasized that there is a great difference in making a living and making a life. She always brought out the moral element in every course, creating a sense of values and the establishment of priorities. For example, when she taught history, she didn't just deal with dates, places, people, and events; she showed how God is sovereign in directing the affairs of men and nations. She explained how corruption brings ruin, and how governing by the principles of the Bible brings the blessings of God. When she taught math and science, she showed how the order of creation is a reflection of divine order. In fact, the very existence of man was the result of the direct creative act of God.

Our school day began with prayer, and Mrs. Reese often read from the Bible, relating all truth to *the Truth* as revealed in God's Word. The government may have thought it was being progressive when it outlawed such things, as well as discipline, but I can remember when we went to school without having to go through a security check, without the presence of armed guards, and without worrying about the possibility of being gunned down. It appears to me that we've got a strange idea of progress.

Even though most of the older boys in school towered over Mrs. Reese, she wasn't afraid to administer discipline to anyone. In addition to receiving my share of paddle sessions, many times I was on the receiving end of a willow switch about five feet long that had a snap like a whip, and stung like one. At least the paddling or the whipping was quickly over, but when you had to stand on one foot in a corner, facing the wall, the punishment seemed to drag on forever. I'm better for the discipline, and I wonder if our teachers today ought not be allowed the freedom to dispense some of the same.

Along with everybody else in those days, Mrs. Reese was a firm believer in castor oil. Any student who was absent from school because of sickness could expect a visit from her that very day. The first time she visited, she brought the castor oil and a vile tasting concoction called 666, an appropriate name if it signifies evil. Anyway, according to Mrs. Reese's diagnosis, the patient received a dose of one or the other. The purpose of her second visit was to see how the sick child was getting along, and believe me, the afflicted kid was doing some fervent praying that when Mrs. Reese laid her hand on his or her brow, there would be no fever. Nothing made us want to get up and go back to school more than the thought of another dose of castor oil or 666. And Mrs. Reese always visited at least three times! I'll tell you this, though—to this day I'm still a believer in the restorative power of castor oil, and I still take it for all kinds of ills.

Mrs. Reese was the daughter-in-law of the Matt Reese who accompanied Granny's family and the others when they came to Texas from Alabama. I last saw her in 1995, not too long before she died, and she was still bossing me around, admonishing me to get my diploma.

Mrs. Reese was a great lady, and she taught her students dignity. She spoke the word *Negro* like it was a title of royalty, and she made us proud of our race. She couldn't understand substitutes like "African-American" or "Black," because she felt like they were poor and shameful apologies for who we are. When I last saw her, once more she told me, "Just say 'Negro,' Charles."

I suppose all of us carry around memories of unforgettable characters who've made impressions on us when we were children. My favorite such memory is that of Uncle Pat Gray. He wasn't really my uncle, or anybody's uncle as far as I know, but that's what we all called him. He was the Uncle Remus of our area, except his stories had the ring of truth, being based on his own experiences. All the children were drawn to him like a moth to the light. He was a tall, bony, light-skinned Negro who carried himself with a military bearing, even though he was stooped with the weight of almost 90 years. He actually had fought alongside his master in the Civil War, with the South, of course. To a wide-eyed boy not quite ten years old, his little two-room house might as well have been the Smithsonian, for all the treasures it contained. I never tired of looking at his collection of swords, still shiny and sharp, pistols, rifles, Minie balls, and other war memorabilia. I cherish this man's memory, because he not only entertained us with stories, but he inspired us with moral teachings. Furthermore, he saved my life.

Severe storms and tornadoes were common happenings in our part of Texas, and a lot of people had built storm cellars where they would take refuge when the weather was threatening. We didn't have a shelter, but Uncle Pat, who lived close by, did. On one occasion when I was about eight years old, the sky darkened and the wind howled. The lightning was terrifying, the thunder was deafening, and we knew a massive storm was building. So Mama herded us all toward the safety of Uncle Pat's storm cellar. I was running at top speed, barefoot as usual, when I stepped on something firm but soft and immediately felt a sharp burning pain in my ankle. I had disturbed a coiled copperhead snake that showed its displeasure by sinking its fangs into my offending foot and depositing its deadly venom into my system. I hobbled the remaining yards to the cellar, wailing for all I was worth. Within seconds Uncle Pat had his Case knife out and commanded Mama and a couple of the girls to pin down my flailing arms and thrashing legs. Then he used his own shirt to tie a tourniquet around my leg below the knee. With all that weight holding me down, especially Mama's, I was so worried about breathing that I hardly felt anything when Uncle Pat slit open my flesh over the snakebite. I probably wouldn't have anyway, since he had cut off my circulation. Without hesitation he started sucking blood and poison out of the wound. Finally, he applied a poultice that he made out of clay and vinegar to help draw out any remaining poison. I guess my racing heart had already pumped some of the poisoned blood into my system, because the next morning my leg was swollen at least three times its normal size from my knee to my foot, and I had a high fever. It took me a week to recuperate, but there's no telling what might have happened without Uncle Pat's quick action. I still have a proud scar that reminds me of him every time I pull on my socks.

There are countless others I could mention who have blessed me in some way. I know that God is the One who takes care of us, but I think He must do most of that kind of work through human instruments. He uses us to help one another, to comfort, to instruct, to provide, to listen. I couldn't possibly recount all the times that the right person was there at the right time, exactly the one I needed at the moment I was in need. Some of you have been among them, and I especially want to thank my loyal fans who have supported me through the years. Many of you have often gone out of your way to attend my performances, and I have been the recipient of innumerable acts of kindness. You have made my career worthwhile, and I thank you sincerely.

CHAPTER ELEVEN

TEARING DOWN WALLS

Although I deliberated at length whether or not to include this chapter, I've determined the situations I relate here are part of my experience, and the views I express describe the way I feel about certain things. I write in love, without any bitterness at all, and with the hope of effecting peace and reconciliation among God's people.

On a scorching summer afternoon in 1950 The Loving Five stopped at a service station in Lubbock, Texas, to get some gas on the way to a performance. A car with out-of-state tags pulled up to one of the pumps. Inside were a man and his wife and three children, the oldest of whom was a little girl about six. It was obvious that they had been travelling a long way, and they were tired and thirsty. The children were fussy and wanted some water. There was a water fountain at the station, but there was also a slight problem. The family who had just driven in was black, and there was no separate fountain designated for "colored." Unless you are over the age of 50 and are from the South, you may not be able to comprehend what I am describing.

Those were the days of segregation, and there were separate facilities, when they existed, for the two races.

The father was a paying customer at the gas station, and he was from a state that allowed him to drink from the same water fountain as anybody else. How was he going to explain to his little children why they couldn't get a drink of water? He didn't want to cause any trouble, yet at the same time he wanted to relieve the thirst of his children. He solved the dilemma by walking with meek dignity over to the drink machine. He picked up an empty Coke bottle from the case on the ground, then took the bottle to the fountain, where he rinsed it out and filled it with cool water. He then gave each of the children a drink. If they had wanted to answer the call of nature, they would have had to pull off the road somewhere and go behind the bushes.

I could identify with that situation, because I was born and grew up in a segregated society, where as "colored" we were expected to know our place and stay there. My closest playmates when I was a child were white twins named Alvin and Calvin. We were together every day, and I spent many nights at their house, sleeping between them on a feather mattress. Then the time came for us to start to school, and I was surprised to find that we would not be going to the same school. For the first time my mother told me about the race problem. I learned very early the boundary lines that prejudice drew around us, and I accepted the system along with everybody else, because that's just the way it was. We could go to the county fair or to the zoo, but only on one designated day of the week. We could shop at Woolworth's, but we couldn't sit at the counter and order anything to eat or drink. We could go to the Grand Theater to see a movie, but we had to use the side entrance in the alley and sit in the very back of the balcony. We could ride a train, but we had to wait for it in a room at the depot designated for the use of "colored." And when we boarded the train, we sat in a coach especially reserved for us. If it was a long trip, we had better have our own sandwiches, because we were not allowed to enter the train's dining car.

Supposedly, the schools in Lamar County, as well as throughout the South, were "separate but equal." That meant, of course, that the "colored" children enjoyed the same educational advantages as the whites. However, the reality of the situation was far different, and the "equal" part was so ludicrous that I won't even comment. Mrs. Reese truly did a marvellous job with all eight grades in her little one-room school.

We worked at whatever jobs we could find, mostly on the farm or at menial tasks involving hard, unskilled labor. The boss was almost always white, and the concept of equal pay for equal labor was a joke. We knew where the line was drawn and we knew not to cross it. We also knew that we were to bear slurs, taunts, insults, and other forms of abuse without retaliation. Two incidents from my boyhood are particularly etched in my mind. I was about ten years old, working in the fields chopping cotton. Now let me explain that term for those of you who have been blessed by never having had the experience. Picture a field of many acres, with a hundred straight rows of young cotton plants, as long as the eye can see. Under the blistering July sun workers with hoes are struggling to loosen the soil and chop out weeds and crowded plants. They trudge the endless rows, heads down, from dawn to dusk, attacking the stubborn earth. There was only a brief respite at noon to break the monotonous routine. It was torturous work, especially for a boy whose thoughts were directed toward the swimming hole or a productive fishing spot.

That was the situation in which the white boss found me one day. I have to admit that my heart wasn't dancing to the tune of a dozen hoes striking the earth, and my efforts were begrudgingly slow. Likely in my dawdling daydreaming I cut out some healthy plants, while overlooking some weeds and leaving some dirt clods untouched by my blade. Anyway, for whatever reason, the boss tied into me. He pulled me around and shoved me to the ground. Then he grabbed me by my shirt and jerked me to my feet. To say he was angry would be a gross understatement. If the scene had not been so serious, I'm sure it would have been comical. He towered over me by at least two feet, but, still clutching a fistful of my shirt, he bent down until only two inches separated his grotesquely furious face from my own terror-stricken countenance. I thought he was going to beat me to death right there. Instead, with his veins threatening to pop out of his neck and his spittle punctuating his words, he embarked on a tirade of derogatory insults directed specifically to me, but generally to all the no-account, lazy, dumb little n—— bastards that infested the world. My mother was only a few feet away, but she could say or do nothing, lest we lose our only means of a livelihood.

About a year later, when I was raking hay with a crew, the boss's son got mad at a friend of mine and started berating him. He wasn't joking when he pulled out a gun and threatened to shoot him, because he knew he could get by with it. There could be no retaliation in such a situation, because in the society in which we lived, the black person always bore the blame, regardless of the circumstances. Some of the typical jokes circulating at that time illustrate the attitude that I'm trying to describe. One story told about the discovery of the body of a black man. His hands were bound behind his back and there were 6 gunshot wounds and 14 stab wounds in his body. The sheriff made a thorough investigation before announcing that it was the worst case of suicide he had ever seen. Another story told about a carload of white hooligans who deliberately ran down two Negro youths walking along the side of the road. The impact was so forceful that one of the youths was knocked into a field about 60 feet away, while the other one crashed through the windshield of the car. When the sheriff arrived and surveyed the scene, he charged the one boy with leaving the scene of an accident and the other one with breaking and entering. I can't repeat some of the more sordid stories.

During the days of my boyhood, in the midst of racial oppression, my mother and grandmother taught me dignity and self-esteem, and that people should judge a person by what he is, not by his color. They impressed upon me the fact that insulters show their ignorance and littleness, and that I should reject the rejection. Gradually, I began to understand that people who harbor or exhibit prejudice are worse off than the object of their bigotry.

At times I wondered how much Granny remembered from her childhood years. Whatever life in Africa was like in the mid-nineteenth century, it was at least a life of freedom and equality. Sometimes I imagined her as the daughter of a powerful chief, with comparative wealth in the village. I pictured her and her playmates frolicking among their simple huts without fear and knowing nothing of prejudice. Perhaps it was from drawing on her own memories of such a life that she was able to instill in me a sense of my own worth as a human being.

I must not leave the impression that all white people looked upon us as inferior and treated us disrespectfully. There were untold acts of mutual kindness between the races, some of which I have already described. In addition, I had many white playmates, particularly the twins Alvin and Calvin.

Unfortunately, the open hostility toward me and other Negroes continued. Many times I was refused service in restaurants, usually with the explanation, "We don't serve n——s here." That statement spoke volumes, none of it worth reading. As an individual I possessed the rights, but I wasn't given the rights. Through the years the police would often stop the car in which we were travelling, for no other reason than it was occupied by a group of black people. We bore their humiliating intimidation silently, because to complain would have invited physical punishment. Most often the officers would laugh through these episodes, making jokes of them. There were even numerous occasions when shots were fired at the motel where we were staying. We learned to handle such situations by making light of them, even to the point of joking about them ourselves.

Even in my professional career I have often been the object of prejudice, most evident in booking arrangements. There have been occasions when some groups refused to appear on the same program with us, or at least made inordinate demands for certain conditions to be met, usually regarding billing and fees. However, the Lord has a way of handling such matters, and I'm a firm believer in Romans 8:28. One time, promoters in a certain city in Georgia, bowing to pressure, rescinded an invitation to The Revivers to appear with other groups at a regional music festival. The thought that our presence might cause some tension, resulting in bad publicity, was the explanation given. This development so upset one of our supporters, who was white, that he personally arranged a concert for us in the same city. Our concert's attendance far exceeded the number that had attended the other program. Not long afterwards we returned to the same city by popular demand, and the attendance was even larger. Many white pastors have confessed to me that they would like to invite me to their churches, but they couldn't for fear that they would be kicked out.

In the mid-'90s I was nominated to receive the Flame award for the best album of the year in recognition of *Let's Have Church* and because The Revivers were the top singing group. Representatives from an internationally known magazine had contacted me regarding writing a feature article about me and printing my picture on their cover. However, I learned from a credible source that someone maneuvered the situation and convinced them that as a black man I was out of my element in Southern Gospel music.

Prejudice doesn't hurt me; it only hurts the person who holds it. I simply refuse to be bothered by it, because it's not worth having my peace and joy disrupted by a sullen spirit of bitterness. Besides, Jesus taught us to bless those who curse us and to pray for them (see Mt. 5:44; Rom. 12:14; 1 Pet. 3:9). Having spoken the words, He set a worthy example for us to follow, because when revilers hurled insults at Him, He did not respond in kind; instead He let God handle the situation (see 1 Pet. 2:23). Furthermore, the Bible tells us that as far as possible we are to "live peaceably with all men" (Rom. 12:18). By nature a hopeless division exists among people. Outside of Christ mankind is a mass of prejudice, resulting in distrust and disharmony. The same kind of racial prejudice that characterized Jews and

Gentiles in the ancient world still infests modern society. People do not hesitate to dismiss with sarcasm and scorn entire groups, nations, or races. The outward symptoms of that kind of attitude betray something lurking deep in the life of a person. People can put on a show and keep up appearances, while beneath there is contempt and loathing, and the mere fact that they are smiling and shaking hands does not necessarily tell you anything about their hearts. An outward display of courtesy or politeness often covers up curses in the inner person.

But racial disharmony is not God's purpose for His creation, and in order to attain the unity that He wants us to have, there must be a radical change in our very natures. It is a sheer waste of time to talk about racial harmony apart from new life in Jesus Christ. Sin has broken human fellowship, and it will continue to fracture it no matter how desperately people without Christ struggle to achieve a relationship of love and trust and service among themselves. Certainly it will not come through legislation or slogans of good will. Attitudes can't be changed until hearts are changed. Without Jesus Christ human fellowship is like dough without yeast or like a lightbulb without electricity. An important ingredient is missing. The only mortar that can hold people together in loving fellowship is the mortar mixed with the blood that Christ shed at the cross. The death of Jesus not only changes individual lives; it brings into being a new society of redeemed people in which former enmities are broken down.

It's a beautiful truth that "there is neither Jew nor Greek, there is neither slave nor free, there is neither male nor female; for you are all one in Christ Jesus" (Gal. 3:28). This statement means to me that in Christ the things that naturally divide us, such as race, rank, and gender, are no longer barriers to fellowship. Certainly in God's sight there is no distinction of race. His promise of salvation includes all nations of every race, color, and language. All of us are equal—equal in our need of salvation, equal in our inability to earn it, and equal in the fact that God offers it to us freely through faith in Christ. Once we have received salvation, that equality is transformed into a fellowship, a brotherhood that only Christ can create.

Galatians 3:28 also tells us that there is no distinction of rank or social status. I reckon that just about every society in the history of the world has developed some kind of class or caste system. Circumstances of birth, wealth, privilege and education have divided people from one another. But in Christ snobbery is prohibited and class distinctions are removed. I'm the son of sharecroppers, born and raised in dire poverty, with not even a high school diploma, but I'm also a son of God, on an equal standing with kings and presidents.

This verse also proclaims that there is no distinction of gender. It asserts that in Christ male and female are one and equal, a pronouncement declared centuries in advance of the times. I understand that Paul wrote these words at a time when women throughout the world were regarded as nothing more than property, and were exploited and ill-treated.

It's obvious that when we become Christians we don't lose our racial, cultural, or sexual identities. I'm still black; you may be white or brown or yellow. I'm still a man, and my background will always be one of poverty. Every person belongs to a certain race and nation, has been nurtured in a certain culture, and is either male or female. Christ has not abolished these distinctions in the sense that they don't exist. They still remain; they simply don't matter anymore. They cannot separate us from each other so as to prevent fellowship among us. We recognize each other as equals, brothers and sisters in Christ.

Truly, right here on earth we would have a foretaste of the fellowship of Heaven if we just practiced the attitude of Jesus in relating to each other. Of course, earth is not Heaven; it's the getting-ready place. And if we don't get along here, what isolated ghettos will we be able to find in Heaven?

Sometimes I believe that there is a curse on this great country that can only be broken as godly people intercede in earnest prayer. America has a lot of repenting to do. There will always be sick, misguided people apart from Jesus Christ. God created only two people; mankind made the rest. All the ills of society come from sin, and we all need to ask God to search our hearts, reveal to us what may be hidden there, and genuinely repent.

Racial tension in this country reached its shameful breaking point in the year 1963. Events focused on Birmingham, Alabama, where a federal court had ordered the schools to be integrated. I was in the city during the first week of May that year, when black demonstrators, joined by a few whites, participated in a peaceful "Children's Crusade" for equality. I personally witnessed the violence that erupted as police attacked both adults and children with powerful fire hoses and vicious snarling dogs. They arrested hundreds of demonstrators. My heart was sick that night, and only the grace of God protected me from the hatred that sought to possess me. I knew that neither the police nor the taunting citizens were the real perpetrators of the crime, and that the true battlefield was not the streets of Birmingham. The warfare was "against principalities, against powers, against the rulers of the darkness of this age, against spiritual hosts of wickedness in the heavenly places" (Eph. 6:12). I spent a lot of time in serious prayer that night.

I was in Birmingham again later that year, at the Sixteenth Street Baptist Church. Two weeks later, on the quiet Sunday morning of September 15, four innocent little black girls were preparing for Sunday school in the basement of that very church. In the same basement was a bomb planted by extreme segregationists, designed to kill and maim and destroy. The explosion took the lives of Denise McNair, Carole Robertson, Cynthia Wesley, and Addie Mae Collins. Angry blacks rioted and the civil authorities responded with great violence. During the rest of the day, police and civilians alike killed other black youths. The country came very close to a widespread and violent racial warfare, but God especially used a man by the name of Martin Luther King, Jr. to still the cries of outraged black militants demanding vengeance. He himself had displayed the attitude of Christ when his house was bombed in 1956 in Montgomery, Alabama, where he was serving as a pastor. He dispersed a vengeful mob with the words, "We must love our white brothers no matter what they do to us."

I knew both the elder King and his son. I was with Martin, Jr. on various occasions, and we often met for lunch in Atlanta. He was a man of education, wisdom, and self-esteem. In spite of his notoriety, he was very much down-to-earth. It saddens me that even today many people regard King as a troublemaker. Actually, he was the opposite, because his way of dealing with oppression was exactly the way that Jesus taught—nonresistance and nonretaliation. From the outset of his career as the foremost leader of the civil rights movement, he preached peaceful resistance. During the boycott of the Montgomery bus system in 1956, instigated by the arrest of Rosa

ANOTHER RIVER TO CROSS

Parks for refusing to give up her seat in the front of a bus, King issued these directions to the black people of the city: "If cursed, do not curse back. If struck, do not strike back, but evidence love and good-will at all times. If another person is being molested, do not arise to go to his defense, but pray for the oppressor." This was the Sermon on the Mount translated into twentieth-century language, and it summarized King's conviction that freedom could be achieved with peace, friendship, and dignity. He maintained this posture, even when there was a growing call among the country's black population for greater militancy in the pursuit of its rights. To the very end of his life he insisted that nonviolence was the only right way—indeed, the Christian way forward. I never fail to be moved by the eloquent words of his *I Have a Dream* speech, delivered before more than 250,000 people who rallied near the Lincoln Memorial on August 28, 1963:

> *The whirlwinds of revolt will continue to shake the foundations of our nation until the bright day of justice emerges. But there is something that I must say to my people who stand on the warm threshold which leads into the palace of justice. In the process of gaining our rightful place we must not be guilty of wrongful deeds. Let us not seek to satisfy our thirst for freedom by drinking from the cup of bitterness and hatred. We must forever conduct our struggle on the high plane of dignity and discipline. We must not allow our creative protest to degenerate into physical violence. Again and again we must rise to the majestic heights of meeting physical force with soul force.*

Unfortunately, as the years passed, Martin's stand for peace lost popularity. Violence was the prevailing mood among many black youths. Black Power characters became the cult figures of press and television. Riots were more newsworthy than peaceful marches. Except for God's grace and the understanding He gave me, I probably would have been among the militant group. But I know that the peaceful way of Jesus, reflected in the life of Dr. King, is the best way, and no unjust act, whether real or imagined, warrants a reaction of rioting, looting, and destruction. Sometimes when blacks engage in violent demonstrations over an injustice done to one of their own, such as police brutality, I wonder if they would be as incensed if the atrocity had been committed against a white person. Wrong is wrong, and right is right, regardless of the race involved, and prejudice has no place when it comes to resisting evil and promoting good.

I know that there is such a thing as corporate responsibility, but I have difficulty believing that we can blame the troubles of contemporary society on cruelties that one group committed against another group 150 years ago. It seems to me that individual opportunity and individual responsibility deserve more focus than pointing the finger of blame at something that happened ages ago. It's beyond me to think that I can blame the past for my present. We can't change the past, so we should just learn from it, change our attitude, and go on.

It really bothers me to see young black people adopt the attitude that the world owes them something, and to hear them excuse their antisocial and unlawful behavior because their great-great-grandparents were mistreated. There is no excuse for individual wrongdoing or laziness. Excuses are for losers. Those who take responsibility for their actions are the real winners. Everyone has problems and obstacles to overcome, but the real winners meet those challenges head on. The "me first" attitude that demands instant self-gratification on the basis of something for nothing is a poor replacement for the servant attitude that Jesus taught. I honestly believe that if we concentrated more on what we owe to other people than on what is due to us, relationships would be improved instantly, whether in the area of race, employment, or any other feature of daily living.

Nobody owes us a living. What we achieve or fail to achieve depends on what we do or fail to do. We can't choose the circumstances of our birth or childhood, but we can choose the direction we want to go. And we can change anything in our life if we want to badly enough.

I heard one of those heart-touching, human interest stories that serves as a perfect illustration of how the races can get along together. Two elderly ladies, one white and one black, had strokes and were living in a nursing home. The white lady had been a concert pianist, and the black lady had been an accomplished piano teacher, but because of paralysis resulting from the strokes, neither could play the piano. However, their afflictions affected only one side of their bodies, the left side of one and the right side of the other. In other words, they each had the use of one arm. After much prayer and discussion, they decided on a daring experiment. Suppose they sat at the piano and played together, one with the left hand and the other with the right? To their delight, they found that with a little practice they could produce beautiful music together. Soon they were entertaining regularly, not only at their own place of residence, but in other nursing homes, hospitals, schools, civic clubs, and wherever else they were invited.

We can accomplish great things when we act in harmony without the bane of unworthy prejudice. Why do we need further identification if we are all brothers and sisters in the family of God? I don't want to be a black gospel singer performing before an audience of predominantly white people. I just want to be a gospel singer performing before an audience of people who have come to be blessed and to praise the Lord. I do not deny my racial identity, but I had rather rejoice in my spiritual identity, and in the fact that I have brothers and sisters "of all nations, tribes, peoples, and tongues" (Rev. 7:9).

CHAPTER TWELVE

TAKING THE AIN'T
OUT OF SAINT

I 've known both highs and lows in my life, and plenty of each. I understand exactly what the apostle Paul meant when he wrote: "I have learned in whatever state I am, to be content: I know how to be abased, and I know how to abound. Everywhere and in all things I have learned both to be full and to be hungry, both to abound and to suffer need" (Phil. 4:11-12). The next verse explains why he could give such a testimony: "I can do all things through Christ who strengthens me" (Phil. 4:13).

I've had to deal with all kinds of trials through the years, and I praise God that I have endured. The Bible tells us, "Count it all joy when you fall into various trials," because trials bring maturity of character (Jas. 1:2). I may not have learned lessons from difficulties as well as I should have, but I do think that I'm a better man for having experienced them. For one thing, I know the value of hard, honest work and the satisfaction that comes from the conviction that you've done a good job. I have described the poverty of my early years. There is certainly no virtue in being poor for poverty's sake, but there should be no shame either, for dignity cannot be smothered by circumstances. The only shame is a negative and passive acceptance of those circumstances and seeking merely to exist rather than to overcome.

One of my heroes when I was a young man was Satchel Paige, one of the best baseball pitchers of his time. He played for years in the Negro League before the major leagues were integrated, and he was over 40 years old when he finally was given the opportunity to pitch a major league game. This man was a living example of perseverance, and I want to pass on to you the advice that he gave: "Never let the odds keep you from pursuing what you know in your heart you were meant to do."

I know the value of that statement, because I'm living proof that it's true. Outside of Granny and Mama, I had little encouragement as a youngster, I had few resources, and I possessed little in the way of natural talent. But I knew what I was called to do, and I set out to do it with God's help. And I want to tell you that success depends as much on desirability as ability. Most people want to succeed, but very few are willing to exert the effort necessary. In most cases success is 10 percent inspiration and 90 percent perspiration. An athlete doesn't become a champion when he wins the event, but in the hours, weeks, months, and years that he spends in preparation. The victory is just the demonstration of his championship character.

I'm not yet where I want to be, but thank God I'm not where I used to be. It hasn't been an easy road that I have travelled. There haven't been any shortcuts in getting to where I am now, but it's been worth all the effort. Sometimes when the going is easy you better watch out. You may be going downhill. Oftentimes young people ask me how they can get started in a career, whether it's gospel singing or some other field. I always respond by asking them the same question: "What is your priority?" Your priority ought to be to serve God and bring glory to Him, not just to receive fame and money. If you put God first, everything else follows, that is, if you are willing to try. The only thing that guarantees failure is never risking a try, and you'll never know how far you can go until you dare to go too far. Without a risk there is no reward, and taking the first step is what separates those who succeed from those who fail. Reach for a goal that you can never reach without God's help, and see what happens. The worst thing you can do is nothing, and I believe it's better to fail trying than failing to try.

Don't allow yourself to be discouraged by others. Over the years I have found that people are generally more prone to tell you what you can't do than what you can do. Well, while they are just *talking* success, you can actually *demonstrate* it. There are three categories of people in this regard: those who make things happen; those who watch things happen; and those who ask, "What happened?"

I have been asked what legacy I want to leave. I want people to remember my staying power. I have stuck to the things in which I believe. I have held out; I have fought the fight; I have run the race. All through my career I have made an honest effort to help people understand that the only way to really live is in Christ. I know that God has worked through me to reach people who could not be reached in any other way. I have heard many testimonies of husbands and children who never listened to gospel music until they heard me. People have been saved and families have been reconciled through the ministry that God has given me.

Someone once asked, "Which song would you like to be the last one you sing?" Without hesitation I responded, "I'm Waiting for the Messiah." This song expresses the Blessed Hope of every Christian, the Second Coming of Christ. Our goal is to meet Him and experience reunion with our departed loved ones. Meanwhile, we wait with perseverance and faithfulness, and encourage others to join us in getting ready.

Verse 1

There's a train bound for Beulah
There's a voice calling, "Come Aboard"
There's a train bound for Beulah
There's a voice calling, "Come Aboard"
It's conducted by the Messiah
He said, "There's room for many more"

Verse 2

I been waiting for a long time
But I'm not tired yet
I been waiting for a long time
But I'm not tired yet
When I make my flight to Beulah
I'll have plenty of time to rest

Verse 3

I'm going to join the family circle
That was broken long ago
I'm going to join the family circle
That was broken long ago
When we reunite in Beulah
It won't be broken anymore

Chorus
I'm waiting for the Messiah
I believe He's soon to come again
I'm waiting for the Messiah
I believe He's soon to come again
When my waiting days are over
I'm gonna shout in Beulah land

The Revivers recorded a video of this song early in the summer of 2000. It seemed everything was against us on the day of the filming. The leaden skies had already poured out their fury on northwest Florida and were threatening an even greater demonstration of their anger. This was the only date we could bring everybody and everything together out of a busy schedule, and Javetta Saunders, who was producing the tape, had already made preparations in the charming little railroad town of De Funiak Springs, Florida. Aside from the weather, satan tried to sabotage the project by causing a mix-up in the rental of the tuxedos we were to use for the filming. Only Javetta's last-minute heroics made order out of the chaos. Still, we were a forlorn company as we sheltered together from the driving rain, while the lightning flashes and thunder peals challenged every bit of faith we had. All we could do was pray for a break in the weather, believing that if Jesus silenced a fierce storm at the Sea of Galilee, He could surely blow away a few thunderclouds in Florida.

And He did! Contrary to every weather report, the storm cleared in our area, and we were able to go through the day's shootings unhurriedly. However, there was still one more hurdle. A major scene in the video was to be the arrival of a train, and officials had assured Javetta that it would be on time. So we waited. And waited. And waited some more. For several hours. Soon it would be too dark to

The Revivers

film, and furthermore, the clouds were threatening to take vengeance against the interruption of their activity. I had not wanted to see a locomotive so much since I saw my first one at the age of six in Paris, Texas. We were taping a video of "I'm Waiting for the Messiah," and it was beginning to look like He would come before the train did. In fact, things looked so hopeless that the director, Miller Goodman, gathered up the equipment and prepared to leave. We decided to pray once more before leaving, and before the prayer was finished we heard the beautiful sound of a train whistle. Miller frantically rushed to get the camera and other necessary equipment. Needless to say, we finished the production of a powerful witness to the glory of Christ. When God wants you to do something, He will provide all the resources necessary for you to do it. Just have faith to persevere.

I haven't arrived yet, and there is still much more that I want to accomplish. I really believe that the strongest part of my ministry is yet to come. At least I know this, that there is no end to a ministry into which God calls you. That ministry endures until the last breath you draw. In continuing my own ministry, I want to gain the confidence of young people through music, so I can show them that there is a difference in satan's realm and the Lord's work. I want to convince them that if they would only trust God and seek His Kingdom first, they won't have to worry about material things. As for myself, I desire a more personal knowledge of God, more wisdom to reach people, and a greater anointing to inspire people and to glorify Christ.

Because I have been singing professionally for so long, some people may call me a "has-been." Well, I'd rather be a has-been than a might-have-been. A might-have-been has never been, but a has-been was once an is. I've had a lot of experiences, and God has been so good to me through the years that sometimes I think it might be a case of mistaken identity.

I know God isn't finished with me yet. On March 16, 2001, in Muskogee, Oklahoma, I had one of the most vivid dreams I have ever had. I know it was from God. In the dream Jesus was talking to me. I didn't see His face, for I was viewing the scene from behind Him as He was speaking to me. People were in a temple that was only partly finished, while construction was still proceeding. The meaning of the dream became clear to me. We, God's people, are the temple. It isn't finished yet, because there are still people who need to be brought in. I'm one of the builders, part of the construction team, and there is work yet to be done.

I'm happy with my life, but not content, for the day that I am content, my dreams will cease to exist. I remember asking my grandmother what she did and how she felt when she realized that she had been set free from slavery. She responded, "Why, chile, when you set free, you got to sing freedom's song." Well, I have been set free to sing, and as long as I have breath, I intend to keep singing freedom's song. The story of Granny's song for freedom struck a chord in the musical heart of Javetta Saunders, so she composed a song that describes the way every true child of God feels. Every time I sing this song, it will be with sincere gratitude to God and in honor of my precious grandmother, who taught me what physical and spiritual freedom mean.

Verse 1

When Moses was down in Egypt,
He led God's people out.
They crossed over to the other side
And began to sing and shout.

Moses said, "Remember our God.
You're no longer a slave to man,
For the new path you're travelling now
Will lead you to the Promised Land."

Chorus

Now I am set free to sing
Glad praises to the King.
I'm no longer a slave, thank God.
I now am saved.
When ole Satan tries to stop me,
I just keep giving praises to the King,
And remind him of the day
I was set free to sing.

Verse 2

I once was a slave to sin
And found no peace within.
There was darkness all around—
For years I'd been bound.
Then a light shined upon me—
My eyes were opened; now I can see.
That's when I was
Set free to sing.

AFTERWORD

As I have already indicated, Charles Johnson is a very modest man, and it was very difficult getting him to talk about himself, even though he was most eager to cooperate. I learned during the writing of the book that much of his desire to tell his story was to fulfill a promise he had made to his Aunt Sweet. She wasn't really his aunt, but she was very much a part of the family, having been raised from infancy by his grandmother as though she were her own child. As she lay dying, Aunt Sweet sent word to Charles to come to her. When he arrived, she presented him with Granny's precious Bible, which had been in her possession since that dear saint died. In addition, she reviewed the family history, starting with the time that Granny and Sarah were sold into slavery. Much of the early history related in this book comes from her account of those events. Then with the final light of life in her eyes, Aunt Sweet solemnly charged Charles to keep this story alive for posterity. This book, in large measure, is the result of the promise that he gave in response.

It was only after the manuscript was completed that Javetta Saunders suggested that I read some of the letters that Charles receives, with the possibility that I might find some material to incorporate in the book. The fact that he receives fan mail never entered my mind, and in actuality, he doesn't. The hundreds of letters that people address to him are more in the nature of testimonies, and they come from all over the world. I knew that Charles makes a tremendous impact on audiences everywhere he appears, but when I read a number of these testimonies, I realized that he is a minister in the fullest sense of the word, even though he has never been officially ordained as a preacher. Perhaps he should be called a music evangelist!

It would be out of order to spend a lot of pages recounting the stories that the letters tell, but I believe readers would appreciate knowing something of the way God has used Charles to change lives. In addition to expressing appreciation for his music and the blessings it imparts, most every letter comments on the way that he relates to people on their level. "Your music tells it the way it is," one writer stated. "It's not designed to impress people but to bless them." Some of the letters follow personal telephone calls that their writers had made to Charles, and invariably they speak of being overwhelmed by his humble willingness to spend time with them in conversation. A letter from a lady in Australia is typical. She knew Charles and The Revivers only through their recordings, which she declared "can make you feel like you belong in the Kingdom of God." Wanting more information, she placed a trans-Pacific call, thinking that she "would be talking to the receptionist or some agent." When she realized that she was talking to Charles, she became very excited, scarcely believing that she "would ever get this close to Charles Johnson himself."

She then wrote of her gratitude that he would "show the love of God to total strangers who are just common people."

Many letters are from wives and mothers praising God for the salvation of husbands and children who were converted through Charles' ministry. One letter from Tennessee reads, "My husband would never attend a church service, because he thinks they are filled with hypocrites, including the pastors. But he likes music, so he came to your concert with me. Every song brought conviction upon him, especially those that warned of waiting too late and facing judgment. When the group sang 'It's Gonna Rain,' he was actually trembling. Then when you spoke and sang of God's love and grace, especially in 'We Cannot Stand Alone,' I saw something I never expected to see. Tears were spilling from his eyes, and he broke down completely. Right there in his seat he cried out to Jesus to save him."

A young pastor wrote to tell about his mother, who was so hardened to the gospel that she had never even come to hear him preach and would get angry when he tried to witness to her. However, she was completely and demonstratively delivered during a Revivers' concert, so much so that she began to shout and dance down the aisle. The pastor concluded, "I know God did it, but without you speaking and singing what God told you, my mom would still be on the way to hell." Testimonies like that are priceless!

I was particularly touched by a card and enclosed letter from a woman in Murfreesboro, Tennessee, whose mother was in the final stages of colon cancer. She stated that her mother was one of Charles' "biggest supporters and admirers," and that she played his tapes "throughout the years, in times of rejoicing and sorrow, of praising Him and in lifting up others in prayer." She continued by saying,

"She is never happier than when she is listening to your music. We see the Holy Spirit all over her face as she lifts her hands in praise while singing along with you." Then she described how she watched as her mother was listening to her favorite song, Charles' recording of "I Can't Even Walk without You Holding My Hand." "She sat there listening to this song, and although she was in physical pain, the words of your song took her away from that, and she lifted her hands in praise, the tears rolling down her face, and she was totally removed for a few minutes of anything related to this world."

I was so moved by this testimony that I called the home and talked to the cancer victim's husband, who added his own expression of appreciation for Charles to that written by his daughter. He also told me that they had received a personal telephone call from Charles in response to the letter and that he had sung to his wife over the phone, prayed with her, and greatly encouraged her. He had also sent them his latest tapes and other items associated with his ministry. Such action is in total accord with the character of Charles Johnson. The daughter's final statement in her letter is a fitting benediction: "God bless you as He uses you to continually spread His joy and His love."

I have absolutely no artistic ability of any kind, and I have a high appreciation for those who do have it. Sometimes there is even the temptation to be envious, but then I realize that God has gifted all of us in some way. How would it be if each one of us were as diligent and enthusiastic as Charles Johnson in developing and using what God has given us!

Jerry Horner

To arrange bookings or to order products, contact:

Charles Johnson
1223 Theodore Lane
Durham, NC 27703
Telephone: 919-596-1731
FAX: 919-596-5740
Email: cbj1606@juno.com

You are welcome to visit Charles Johnson's website at:

charlesjohnson.homestead.com

Additional copies of this book and other book titles from DESTINY IMAGE are available at your local bookstore.

For a complete list of our titles, visit us at www.destinyimage.com Send a request for a catalog to:

Destiny Image® Publishers, Inc.

P.O. Box 310
Shippensburg, PA 17257-0310

"Speaking to the Purposes of God for This Generation and for the Generations to Come"